A SU … LENTY

This is the story o… …onal summer enjoyed by the Yorkshire cricketer **G… …erbert Hirst** in 1906. A popular and wholehearted charact…, one of the greatest all-rounders in the history of the game, he achieved that summer the unique feat of scoring 2,000 runs and taking 200 wickets in one season.

Some of the proceeds raised from the sale of this book are being donated to the Yorkshire County Cricket Club's Archives Committee, which has been set up to preserve and celebrate the cricketing heritage of the county.

Stephen Chalke has written several books on cricket, including *No Coward Soul – The Remarkable Story of Bob Appleyard* (co-written with Derek Hodgson and chosen as Wisden Book of the Year 2004), *At the Heart of English Cricket – The Life and Memories of Geoffrey Howard* (Cricket Society Book of the Year 2001) and his latest title *Ken Taylor – Drawn to Sport*.

Fairfield Books is a specialist publisher of cricket books. For full details of all its titles or to be added to its mailing list, please write to **17 George's Road, Bath BA1 6EY** or telephone **01225-335813**.

Fairfield Books
17 George's Road, Fairfield Park, Bath BA1 6EY
Tel 01225-335813

Copyright © Stephen Chalke
Page and cover design by Niall Allsop

First published 2006
ISBN 0 9544886 5 2

Printed and bound in Great Britain by
Bath Press, Bath

A SUMMER OF PLENTY

George Herbert Hirst in 1906

STEPHEN CHALKE

FAIRFIELD BOOKS

Preface

This book has been written as part of Yorkshire County Cricket Club's celebration of the centenary of George Herbert Hirst's remarkable summer of 1906. The club's recently formed Archives Committee has given me great encouragement and support, and I am delighted that Yorkshire, a county with such a rich cricketing tradition, should now be looking after its history with so much care. Some of the proceeds of this book are going to support the work of the Archives Committee. So it is to be hoped that there will be further such celebrations in the years to come.

It has been a delight to research and write this book. It is a happy subject and, as I have typed the words, I have felt the warmth of George Hirst's smile, his kindly presence bringing joy to me just as he brought joy to so many cricket lovers all those years ago. We live in a more sophisticated world, and in many ways we have made our cricket a more complicated game. So it is inspiring to reach back across time and to touch the human spirit of a man who, within his own era, without all the advantages of modern life, could sustain his great skills so untiringly across such a long summer. He achieved extraordinary numerical returns for his labours, but he did not play for those personal returns. He played for his team, and he loved nothing more than the challenge of a crisis. In an age when county cricket was keenly fought and attracted great crowds, he was considered by many to be the greatest of all county cricketers, and it may be that, one hundred years on, he still is.

In researching and writing this book, I have had help from many people, and I would like to thank Bob Appleyard, Margaret and Ronnie Ashton, Ron Deaton, Sidney Fielden, Barry Johnston, Ted Lester, Ruth Lyles, Pat Neal, William Roberts, Chris Saunders, David Smith, Lindsay Watkins and David Wilkinson. In their different ways they have all guided me towards material that has made it possible to write this story. I would especially like to thank Ron Deaton for his careful reading of the text.

Inevitably, with the events of the book a hundred years away and the subject dead for over half that time, it has been necessary to draw in the main on written material. I have made full use of the *Yorkshire Post* and *The Times*, and I have occasionally referred to other local newspapers. I have consulted the magazine *Cricket – A Weekly Record of the Game* and *Wisden Cricketers' Almanack*, and I have had access to some pamphlets, benefit brochures and letters. I have used as invaluable reference sources the CricketArchive website and the *Who's Who of Cricketers* by Philip Bailey, Philip Thorn and Peter Wynne-Thomas. And, thanks to William Roberts, I have even held in my hand the ball with which George Herbert completed his 'double double'.

I have also read and occasionally quoted from the following books:

John Arlott, *The Great All-Rounders*
Bill Bowes, *Express Deliveries*
Gerald Brodribb, *The Croucher*
James P. Coldham, *Lord Hawke*
Lettice Cooper, *Yorkshire West Riding*
Bill Frindall, *The Wisden Book of Cricket Records*
George Beldham & C.B. Fry, *Great Batsmen: Their Methods at a Glance*
George Beldham & C.B. Fry, *Great Bowlers: Their Methods at a Glance*
C.B. Fry, *A Life Worth Living*
Roy Genders, *League Cricket in England*
Lord Hawke, *Recollections and Reminiscences*
Derek Hodgson, *The Official History of Yorkshire County Cricket Club*
Len Hutton, *Just My Story*
Grenville Jennings, *Yorkshire County Cricketers on Old Picture Postcards*
Gilbert Jessop, *A Cricketer's Log*
J.M. Kilburn, *A History of Yorkshire Cricket*
A.E. Knight, *The Complete Cricketer*
Don Mosey, *We Don't Play It For Fun*
Patrick Murphy, *The Centurions*
Patrick Neal, *George Herbert Hirst – Mirfield Cricket Club 1891*
Cecil Parkin, *Cricket Triumphs and Troubles*
Cecil Parkin, *Parkin on Cricket*
Clive Porter, *Kent Cricket Champions 1906*
A.W. Pullin, *History of Yorkshire County Cricket 1903-1923*
Sidney Rogerson, *Wilfred Rhodes*
Herbert Strudwick, *25 Years Behind the Stumps*
Peter Thomas, *Yorkshire Cricketers 1839-1939*
A.A. Thomson, *Cricket: The Golden Ages*
A.A. Thomson, *Hirst and Rhodes*
P.F. Warner, *The Book of Cricket*
P.F. Warner, *My Cricketing Life*
Anthony Woodhouse, *The History of Yorkshire CCC*
S.M.J. Woods, *My Reminiscences*
Frank Woolley, *The King of Games*

The photographs of George Hirst batting and bowling were taken by George Beldham in 1905 and are reproduced from the Beldham/Fry books listed above. The drawing of the Brown Cow is by Susanna Kendall.

Stephen Chalke
Bath, July 2006

A Summer Without Equal

When, at the North Marine Road Cricket Ground at Scarborough on Thursday 30th August 1906, with his first ball after tea, George Herbert Hirst of Yorkshire took his 200th wicket of the summer, to add to the 2,000 runs he had completed two days earlier in Bath, he became the first cricketer ever to complete the 'double double'.

It was an age when first-class cricket was still in relative infancy. The county championship had been established formally 16 years earlier, and Test matches were intermittent affairs, just 34 of them – all against Australia – staged in England in the previous quarter of a century. Statistical records were being broken with regularity and, though Hirst's summer's work occasioned tributes, there was not then the sense that his record would stand for all time as it has done, a monument of skill, strength and supreme stamina that will almost certainly never be equalled. As the cricket writer FS Ashley-Cooper wrote that autumn, 'Only a person possessed of an iron constitution could have got through the amount of work that he has done.'

'As a bowler,' Lancashire's captain Archie MacLaren wrote, 'he can keep up his pace for a tremendous time, possessed as he is of wonderful physique, and he can follow up a hard day's work by hitting up a century.'

'Like so many Yorkshiremen,' the cricket writer WA Bettesworth wrote, 'he looks as strong as a house, with a firmly knit figure and a vast amount of muscle which never seems to develop into fat. Such a man is not exactly the type of an athlete, but there are few men playing in first-class cricket who would care to take on Hirst for a hundred yards race. At the end of the day, as at its beginning, he seems all energy.'

'The most untiring and enthusiastic cricketer who ever wore flannels,' MacLaren called him. 'The exceptional amount of work he got through, season after season, would have worn out half a dozen men of lesser physique.'

Though the world has moved on, and modern cricketers believe that the game has advanced greatly from that played by their predecessors, it is truly doubtful in this one respect – of great stamina – that anybody playing today could sustain to such a standard of success the schedule that George Hirst undertook in the summer of 1906.

He was 35 years old before the summer was out, and he carried an old knee injury that required him to strap himself up before bowling. Yet day after day, in 18½ weeks between 7th May and 12th September, he batted and bowled with unstinting determination, his efforts punctuated by long train journeys: from Catford to Leeds, from Sheffield to Leyton, from Bath to Scarborough. Every match was crucial, with Yorkshire pressing hard to retain their championship crown, and he was at his best when it mattered most. In 58 innings, despite batting down the order at number five, his tally of runs was 2,385, second in all England to the prolific Surrey opener Tom Hayward. With the ball, despite being a quick bowler who approached the wicket with an energetic, bounding run, he bowled more overs (1,306) and took more wickets (208) than any man.

On only two other occasions in the history of the game has an all-round cricketer topped even 1,700 runs and 170 wickets in a season: George Hirst himself five years earlier and Frank Woolley, a slow left-arm bowler, in 1920. In the modern game, even adding in all the one-day performances, there are so many days off that such figures are far beyond the bounds of possibility.

Not that George Hirst was a man who played for his figures. The Yorkshire captain was Martin Bladen, the seventh Baron Hawke, and he had a system of awarding marks each day, each mark yielding a five-shilling bonus to the professional. 'Never,' he wrote later, 'would I give marks when I could see a man was playing for records which were detrimental to his side winning the match. Fifty runs on a plumb wicket might not be half so valuable to a side as a contribution of twenty on a sticky pitch.' That summer he paid 'Georgie Hirst', as he called him, £52 – 10s, the most he ever paid to one man in a reign as Yorkshire captain that lasted from 1883 to 1910.

'It was not only what Georgie Hirst did,' he wrote, 'but how he did it, coming off when an effort seemed most necessary and playing his best against the more formidable sides. As an all-round man in county cricket there has been no one to surpass him since WG Grace in the 'seventies lifted Gloucestershire to the top of the tree.'

There were some who went further than this. 'Hirst,' wrote the Middlesex leg-break bowler Bernard Bosanquet, 'is the greatest cricketer ever seen, greater even than WG Grace.'

George Hirst was a happy cricketer, a man who commanded the respect of all social classes. "His smile used almost to meet at the back of his neck," Lord Hawke said of him. Or, as Pelham Warner the Middlesex and England captain wrote, 'It does one good to see him laugh. In many ways he is the ideal cricketer, so straight, so strong, so honest. He shared, with Jack Hearne, the distinction of being the most popular and respected professional of the day.'

In the words of AA Thomson, 'He was a plain, honest Yorkshireman, who had the good fortune to possess high skill in a happy, vigorous game. He had, to the highest degree, the virtue that the Victorians called manliness, but without a jot of Victorian sententiousness. To peer, industrialist, working man or timid schoolboy he was always the same: a friendly soul, kindly but sensible, whose genial face, without the least affectation, radiated to the full the happy spirit of the English game.'

'Cricket is a game, not a competition,' Hirst would say. 'And, when you're both a bowler and a batter, you're twice as happy. You enjoy yourself twice as much.'

What fun he must have had in that summer of 1906 – and how much pleasure he must have given. In the whole history of the game, his was a summer without equal.

George Hirst the cricketer

George Herbert Hirst was born on 7 September 1871, in the Brown Cow Inn in the stone-built village of Kirkheaton, less than three miles from the centre of the fast-developing mill town of Huddersfield, on the edge of the wind-swept moors of the West Riding.

His grandfather was both publican and farmer, and he and his wife had nine children, the youngest of whom was born only six months before the eldest – Mary – gave birth to George. She was not at the time married – did not marry for another eight years – so George grew up in the inn in a large family, full of uncles and aunts. According to George's grand-daughter Lindsay Watkins, he was treated as a special child. "His mother always gave him great encouragement. She was very proud of him."

It was a part of England where the people were hardy. Perhaps, in Darwinian terms, the stock had had to be strong to survive. As one guide book of the 1950s put it, 'There are lovely summer days on the moors and on the Pennine slopes, but not many days on which there is no wind blowing. Typical West Riding weather is made up of blowing wind and driving rain. Autumn comes early, and the spring is long and cold. A harsh climate has made extra demands on the endurance of a race who have had to struggle for centuries with poor soil and difficult transport. Such is the warp of the West Riding, the background on which a tenacious people have woven the pattern of their history.'

George Herbert Hirst was nothing if not tenacious. He left school at the age of ten, working first for a hand-loom weaver in the village, then in a dye-works on the other side of the valley. It was not an unhappy childhood, but the physical demands on him gave him in later life an inbuilt sturdiness of body, a solidity of temperament and a never-forgotten gratitude that he could spend his days in the sun, with bat and ball, where others laboured in mills and mines.

In 1879 George's mother married John Berry, a cloth-finisher who has always been understood by the family to be George's natural father. They moved to a small cottage in New Street, Kirkheaton. Up to that point he had grown up in the inn, which was run by his grandmother, in those years when cricket first took hold in the district. The village of Kirkheaton formed a cricket club in the 1860s, and, by the time the young George was showing an interest in the late 1870s, they had moved to their third ground, at Hole Bottom. In 1937 he shared his recollections of those times:

> My early days were spent at the old Brown Cow Inn. There, we boys played our cricket in the yard, and the Intake Field below, next to the old cricket field. We were only allowed in the cricket field if they were short of fielders at practice; otherwise we were chased out after sneaking over the wall.

The Brown Cow

I think the greatest pleasure to boys like myself at that time, was to watch Bill and Joe Hallas, both colliers, sneak short runs. Bill Hallas was a great character, he always ran if possible in the line of the ball – very often he got hit in the back. That, of course, pleased us, and he did not appear to mind. Then there were the Liberals against the Conservatives – Blues and Yellows – great days for us youngsters to sport our colours! Single-wicket matches before breakfast at Whitsuntide for a Ham and Egg breakfast were common in the old days. I often picture the old ground, with field set.

They put canvas round on Saturdays to prevent spectators looking on without paying, but this was impossible.

Then came the new ground on Bank Row. My first connection as member of the club, I think would be about 1885 or 1886 when I joined, but exact dates I'm unable to state. We lads practised cricket, football and knurr and spell every spare moment we could get after work. In fact our parents said we lived on the ground. Practice with the ball makes the player – well, we got our share.

My early days were of the home-made ball, cut-down boots, and the road or quarry for play.

Some say that the loom-owners, for all their religious principles, would bet on the inter-village matches and, as a consequence, were happy to allow their best players time off to practise. Others say that the speed of the shuttle and pick, in those pre-powered days, increased the hand-eye co-ordination of the loom operators. Whatever the reason, a high standard of cricket quickly developed in the area. By 1883 there was a Heavy Woollen District Cup, followed by a Lumb Cup, and in 1888 – when Hirst was 16 – Kirkheaton Cricket Club paid the former Yorkshire professional Allen Hill, taker of Test cricket's first wicket, to coach its youngsters. 'It was the only coaching I ever received,' Hirst said in an interview after he retired.

George Hirst may only have joined the club at the age of 14, but he was winning batting and bowling prizes by the time he was 15, and in 1889, at the age of 17, he was invited to play for Yorkshire in a minor match against Cheshire at the Fartown ground in Huddersfield. "I was a bit nervous," he admitted four years later, "not funky exactly, but I was so well known on this ground, and a few friends turned up specially to see how I should shape up, that it was not to be wondered at if I did next to nothing."

In fact, he took three for 35 in 22 overs in the Cheshire first innings, and two years later – having learnt much as a 'Saturday man' at the more prominent Elland and Mirfield clubs – he made his championship debut for Yorkshire at Taunton. At this stage he batted in the tail, but his fast left-arm bowling became an established part of the Yorkshire attack when, in the first match of 1893, he took twelve MCC wickets for 48 runs at Lord's. He spoke modestly of his method to the magazine *Cricket* in August of that year:

> No, I've copied nobody and don't intend to now. Not because I think so highly of my bowling, but because if I were to change my style now I might lose the little skill I have.
>
> I always bowl fast, never put in a slow one, taking care not to bowl beyond my strength. The fact is, any slows I might send down would be sure to be knocked all over the place.
>
> This year has been best, and I am delighted that our county is right up at the top. But I want to do better still. Shouldn't I like to turn out a second Tom Emmett!

Emmett, also a left-arm fast bowler, was the greatest character at that point in Yorkshire's cricketing history. A happy man, with a comically large nose and a stream of witticisms, he was so popular that, when no suitable gentleman was available, he became the county's captain for five years.

Yet George Hirst, for all his steady success in the 1890s, would not have equalled Emmett's record of success if his bowling had not acquired its extraordinary 'swerve' in 1901. 'Before this season,' Pelham Warner wrote, 'Hirst had been just an ordinary good fast left-handed bowler, but he learnt to swerve the ball and he jumped at once into the front rank of bowlers. He made the ball swerve in the last two or three yards of its flight, and though this was a good year for batsmen he took 183 wickets.'

'There is nothing imaginary about this swerve,' CB Fry wrote. 'Hirst can bowl a ball which during the first half of its flight is travelling so that if it kept straight on in the air it would pass a foot outside the off stump, but which in the last half of its flight swings in enough to pitch on the middle stump and pass outside the legs of a right-hand batsman.'

'He can clean beat the greatest bat,' Lancashire's captain AC MacLaren wrote, 'when that lightning-like swerver on the off stump rips up the pitch and sends the leg peg flying.'

Bob Appleyard, the great Yorkshire and England bowler of the 1950s, attended Headingley as a schoolboy in 1939 and was shown by Hirst how to swing the ball. Later, in the early 1950s, when he had broken into the Yorkshire team, he called occasionally in winter at the old man's house in Huddersfield. "We'd sit there with two 'pint pots' of tea," Bob recalls. "I always carried a cricket ball in my pocket, and he showed me again how he used to angle the seam in the direction he wanted the ball to swing, so that it would act like a sail on a boat. The trick was to propel the ball through the air without allowing it to revolve. As he was releasing it, he would pull downwards with his hand."

Hirst himself is on record talking about how he worked out his swerve:

> A thing that struck me during my bowling as a young player was that I used to get a lot of wickets with a 'yorker'. I observed that sometimes this 'yorker' used to curl or swerve in the air. This set me thinking there was something in the swerve.
>
> Experience showed me eventually that under certain atmospheric conditions the ball can be made to swerve. The best conditions are where the ground is enclosed with trees, and there is a nice soft breeze, with a little moisture in the atmosphere. The best wind I found was a half-head wind. That is to say, bowling, as I did left arm, the best breeze for the swerve was that which came towards me, say from third man.
>
> It is also a curious fact that after bowling nine or ten overs the swerve disappeared and, with the ball then in use, was no more seen. The newness of the ball having gone, it fails to curve in the air current, and the curious thing about it is that when the swerve goes it goes instantly.
>
> Then there are the days when you naturally expect a ball to swerve but you cannot get the least swerve on it; by the contrary, when you least expect it you get an extraordinary swerve. I used to call the latter my 'funny days', and I don't know a better term for it. It used to baffle me – and I think batsmen also!

At Scarborough, in that summer when he developed his swerve, he bowled out Robert MacDonald of Leicestershire for a duck. MacDonald was an Australian-born dentist who was playing as an amateur, and that evening in the hotel he was not happy. "Well, really," he complained, "I don't know how a batsman can be expected to play a ball that, when it leaves the bowler's arm, appears to be coming straight but, when it reaches the wicket, is like a very good throw from cover point."

Hirst's grand-daughter Margaret, who had been taught to play cricket at Wycombe Abbey School, recalls her grandfather bowling at her one day on the tennis lawn in her back garden. "There I was, all ready with the bat, and the ball came in to me from way out on the off side. I was amazed. It curved so much. It really was a surprise."

The Yorkshire keeper was David Hunter, and he knew better than most the extent of the swerve: "I have seen him make the ball swerve fully four feet time and time again. And this at a beautiful pace and with a splendid length. It was not easy to take this kind of bowling, though not infrequently the stumps saved you the trouble!"

As late as 1906, Hirst's annus mirabilis, the laws only allowed one ball to be used in a complete innings. So, with no modern lacquers to retain the shine, the ball would soon lose its early advantage for the swing bowler. Hirst may have been a pioneer of swing, but he was much more than that. Neville Cardus referred to 'the great ham of his left arm', and there is no doubt that he had strength and stamina in plenty.

'The deadliest of Hirst as a bowler,' wrote the Leicestershire and England batsman AE Knight, 'lies quite as much in his determination as in his deadliest swerve. There is no one in England who so deliberately and persistently bowls for all he is worth, against whom one dare not relax one's vigilance.'

In the summer of 1906 Hirst bowled more than 1,300 overs, and he relied on that determination, that fighting spirit, much more than on an easy run-up and delivery. 'Starting with a sort of hop,' Knight wrote, 'he bounces to the wicket almost as roundly as an india-rubber ball, a wearing, caring action, which takes a great deal out of him.' As WA Bettesworth observed:

> It cannot be said that Hirst's action would ever lead one to suppose that he was a great bowler. He seems to waste so much energy before he reaches the wicket that he ought to be tired out after a dozen overs, if he were built on the lines of ordinary bowlers. In his course to the wicket he reminds one irresistibly of a cork tossed about by little waves on the sea; he bobs up and down until it seems ridiculous to suppose that he can send in an extremely fast ball, and it is only after one has studied him a great deal that one really *expects* to see something out of the common from him in the way of pace.

Not only was he bowling with an awkward run-up, but he was still suffering somewhat from the after-effects of an injury sustained in May 1903 in a disastrous match at Taunton.

The Yorkshire new ball bowlers in that game were Hirst and Jack Brown of Darfield, and both sustained injuries while bowling. Brown threw out his shoulder and was immediately subjected to some gung-ho treatment by Somerset's Australian captain Sammy Woods:

> I took off my boot and tried to put the shoulder in at once but couldn't manage it, although I had someone to sit on his head and others to hold him down. He was very sweaty from bowling, I couldn't get a firm grip of his arm, so he had to go to hospital and have it done. I am certain to this day that had he kept still it would have saved a lot of trouble. Poor fellow, I don't think he ever bowled again.

George Hirst's knee injury was less dramatic but it looked for a while as if the consequences would be as serious.

> I was told by the doctor who attended me that I was 'finished', while a specialist afterwards consulted said I would never be able to bowl again.

A determined man, he travelled to Worcester for the next match where, though he did not bowl, he scored a century. 'Hirst was lame,' *The Times* reported, 'but he batted brilliantly.' He managed three overs in the Roses match at Old Trafford the following week, but it was mid-June before he was back in wholehearted action, bowling more than 700 overs in the remaining 24 matches.

> The knee was always a culprit afterwards, and for years I had to have it bandaged when bowling.

Hirst was a great battler, and in the early years of his Yorkshire career he worked his way steadily up the batting order. 'He was not a graceful batsman,' Bettesworth wrote, 'and not altogether orthodox, but when one watches him, one thinks of all the Australian batsmen of the earlier times, who, though they might not do the ideal thing with a ball, had a habit of "getting there".'

"Right," Hirst would say to the bowler sometimes. "It's either thee or me for it." He loved the contest.

'His style reminded one of a lifeboat coxswain hard at work,' ran his obituary years later in the *Manchester Guardian*. 'It was a mixture of heavy movement and vast heavings, patience until the right ball came along, then a big pull and a strong pull. Hirst's pull was surely the noisiest stroke in cricket.'

'As a batsman,' AE Knight wrote, 'he has qualities which appeal distinctly to popular taste and feeling. Like a big drum, he can be unmistakably seen and heard. Solid as he is, there is a certain eager movement, springy and prancy and buoyant, about his terrific square cut or his sweeping pulls and drives.'

CB Fry summarised him as follows:

> Batsmen of the build of George Hirst, solid and square, are, as a rule, either lacking in freedom or else somewhat ungainly in their strokes. But George Hirst's tremendous square strength is combined with a quite exceptional neatness of foot and suppleness of limb, and the power of his strokes comes not so much from his muscle as from his timing, freedom of movement, and the amount of first-rate wrist-work he puts in.
>
> In many ways his style is almost classical. His cutting and off-driving are in perfect order, and he is a very sound back player. On slow, wet wickets and on difficult, sticky wickets he is one of the most dangerous batsmen living. He watches the ball very closely and is very quick with his bat.
>
> He has one stroke which is unique. He jumps in front of his wicket with both feet together so that he is facing the bowler and lets fly at the ball with a full horizontal sweep of the bat, which, if the stroke is correctly timed, drives the ball to square leg.

In 1904 Hirst became the first Yorkshireman to hit 2,000 runs in a season for his county. These were still years when the ball had to be hit out of the ground for a six to be recorded, yet the following May, at Aylestone Road, Leicester, he made 341, setting a Yorkshire record that still stands a hundred years on. "If it hadn't been for the fielding of their substitute Tom Jayes, who was then a lad of 18, my score would have been 400 or more," he later said. "He saved boundary after boundary, and he got more applause for stopping runs than I did for scoring them."

As a batsman, though, it was as a result of his performance in the famous Oval Test of 1902 that he became a national hero.

He was rarely at his best in Tests "He never liked them," Lord Hawke said, "and he never wanted to play in them." He suffered terribly from both home-sickness and sea-sickness on his two trips to Australia, and his first eight Test appearances yielded him a disappointing six wickets.

Yet three of those six wickets came in dramatic circumstances in the first Test of 1902, the first Test ever to be held at Edgbaston. In 23 spell-binding overs he and Wilfred Rhodes put out the Australians, Victor Trumper and all, for just 36 runs. Rhodes took the lion's share of wickets with seven but, in the view of CB Fry, 'it was Hirst who was responsible for the debacle,' calling it 'the best instance I know of the bowler at the other end getting wickets for his colleague.'

Rain saved the Australians, but they had no such relief when they travelled to Headingley to play Yorkshire in the next match. This time, it was Hirst and Jackson in tandem, and in 14 overs the Australians were all out for 23. Hirst took five for nine, and he always reckoned that the ball with which he bowled Trumper that day was the best he ever bowled.

"He saw all the batsmen from Grace to Hutton," says Margaret Ashton's husband Ronnie, "and he told me that the very best was Victor Trumper. And without doubt the best bowler was Sydney Barnes."

After all this, he was out of the England team by the fourth Test at Old Trafford. According to AA Thomson, 'I well remember – I was eight years old – the convulsive shudder that passed through Yorkshire like a seismic tremor, when the news spread.' In his absence Australia secured an improbable three-run victory and retained the Ashes.

Hirst returned for the final Test at The Oval, where he took five wickets in the Australian first innings. Then, top-scoring with 43, he crucially saved the follow-on and on the final day played his part in a contest that had 22,000 spectators in agonies of suspense. Chasing 263 for victory, England – on a brute of a wet wicket – collapsed to 48 for five. Then, as the pitch calmed down, Gilbert Jessop – the great Gloucestershire hitter – counter-attacked with a 75-minute century. For much of the time he was partnered by the Honourable FS Jackson but, when the latter departed with the score on 157, it was George Hirst's turn and some say that he was lucky to survive a great appeal for lbw off the first ball he faced.

Jessop went at 187, Bill Lockwood – with just two to his name – at 214, and 'Dick' Lilley the wicket-keeper – with 16 – at 248. By then, with Hirst not out on 49, England needed 15 for victory and there was only Hirst's younger Kirkheaton team-mate Wilfred Rhodes to come.

Fifteen to win. 'The score crept up,' wrote one witness, calling himself Country Vicar. 'Whenever the batsmen crossed, the vast crowd thundered its applause. Once, when Hirst hit a two, the Oval seemed to rock with the shouts. The score crept up. The tension grew strained almost to cracking-point. An over was an agony – it took so long. Hirst had a habit of settling his pads between each ball. He would draw his hand up one leg, then up the other. He never failed to carry out that little ritual. He would also pat the ground and remove tiny obstacles. Hirst was taking no chances. No one thought of blaming him – he was saving England – winning the match for the Old Country!'

When scores drew level, 'A parson rushed howling on to the field of play.' Then came the winning hit, hats were thrown in the air, and 'the throng gave vent to their pent-up feelings.'

In the words of AA Thomson, 'That last wicket stand is as encrusted with legends as a bottle of old port with cobwebs.'

Did George Hirst really meet Rhodes with the words, 'We'll get 'em in singles'? Len Hutton wrote that Hirst once told him he did say that, but there does exist a tape in which Hirst as an old man claims that what he said was, 'Play your ordinary game, Wilfred, and we shall win.' But Thomson himself, pressing Hirst for confirmation of the 'get 'em in singles' story, was met only with the answer, "You never remember what you say at times like that."

Whatever the truth, George Hirst – his unbeaten 58 made with an unruffled calm – was a national hero.

Ronnie Ashton, husband to George's grand-daughter Margaret, recalls talking to him about that day. "It must have been wonderful to bat at the other end to Jessop," Ronnie said.

"Oh yes," George replied. "It was." Then quietly he added, with no hint of boastfulness, "I didn't do badly myself."

The writer Alfred Gibson put it as follows:

> Like most great cricketers, George Hirst is frequently seen to greatest advantage in fighting a forlorn hope. When things are looking their blackest, this is Hirst's opportunity. Few will forget his smiling face when he went forth from the pavilion to save England at The Oval. He feels responsibility keenly, but responsibility does not make him sad. He belongs to the optimistic order that infect others with their good spirits. This is probably why Yorkshire as a team have fought and conquered in so many battles against desperate odds.

George Hirst never betrayed his Huddersfield roots, and his years of success on the cricket fields of England owed much to his cheerful temperament and to the extraordinary stamina he developed in his early years at Kirkheaton.

AE Knight, a fellow tourist in Australia in 1903/04, wrote of Hirst:

> The stiff, sturdy solidity of his frame speaks of the wide moors of his home. To look at him after a day in blistering heat, and amid worn, drawn faces, was to feel again the wind-swept wolds, to feel the coolness of the rain upon one's forehead. Australia may produce better cricketers, but her climate forbids the production of a George Hirst.

He grew up in the later years of the Victorian age, in the century before the motor car, the central heating radiator and all the paraphernalia of affluence started to ease the conditions of life in the West Riding. The stock was strong, surviving the wind across the Pennines, the poor soil, the long journeys on foot, and George Herbert Hirst – at work by the age of ten and happily playing in the inn yard and in the fields every evening – was among the strongest.

Team of 1906

J. T. Rothery W. H. Wilkinson W. Rhodes C. H. Grimshaw
S. Haigh J. Tunnicliffe Lord Hawke G. H. Hirst D. Hunter
D. Denton Mr. T. L. Taylor H. Myers

The Month of May

Lord Hawke was Yorkshire's cricket captain that summer, as he had been for the previous 23 summers. He was 45 years old, and he only arrived back in England the week before the season started, having spent three months in India with Prince Ranjitsinhji: "A delightful holiday, spent mostly in game shooting." He returned to his ancestral home, Wighill Park near Tadcaster, with conquests that included a lion, a bison and several panthers.

In an interview with the *Yorkshire Post*, he took issue with proposals being put forward by Essex and Warwickshire that were designed to eliminate drawn games – "There can be no greater pleasure than to see a man with his back to the wall, saying 'You can't get me out!'" – and he condemned the frequent publication of averages in the newspapers: "It does more harm than good, and I wish the Press would help me to suppress it."

In extolling the merits of the 'fighting' draw, he cited the example of the game at Leyton the previous August when Yorkshire, needing only to avoid defeat to win the championship, found themselves following on 423 runs behind Essex. George Hirst batted almost five hours for 90. Then, when he was dismissed, the big-hitting Ernest Smith came in and held out for the final hour for 0 not out. "The most historic and creditable blob in the whole history of cricket," Hawke called it, though *The Times* reported that 'A few spectators, deficient in manners as well as knowledge of the game, repeatedly jeered and Lord Hawke, when he went in, absolutely refused to go on with the innings until the crowd desisted.' "Oh how thankful we felt when the umpires called Time," Hawke wrote. "Never had I been through such hours."

So it was that Yorkshire entered the summer of 1906 as reigning champions, and their warm-up week consisted of a game against 18 Colts at Headingley, followed by a non-first-class match at Cardiff Arms Park against South Wales, a match largely ruined by rain – though not before Yorkshire had bowled out the Welshmen for 50.

May 1906. Statistics revealed that the British Empire now held sway over more than one-fifth of the world's land surface. The new Liberal Government had been elected by a landslide at the start of the year, and David Lloyd George, Chancellor of the Exchequer, was proposing to introduce a means-tested old age pension of up to five shillings a week from the age of 70. A bitter struggle was taking place between Anglicans and Non-Conformists over the funding through the general rates of schools at which only members of the Church of England could teach. And, in response to residents' complaints about the dust thrown up by motor cars, the county council in the West Riding of Yorkshire was considering the use of tar-wash or tar-macadam 'to moderate the nuisance'.

Yorkshire's cricketing summer began with 2½ weeks away from home. After their rain-ruined visit to Cardiff they travelled to Lord's, where they were beaten by a strong MCC side, and from there to Southampton where, in cold weather, they started their championship campaign. It was one of the best wickets in England – one, according to George Hirst, on which 'a good batsman ought to get runs with a walking stick' – but, bowling left-arm round the wicket and 'with a considerable amount of swerve', he took six wickets as the home side were dismissed for 198. Yorkshire's reply of 421 made victory look certain, but on the last day they were held up by an unknown 19-year-old left-hander Philip Mead, who grafted his way to a maiden hundred that was 'heartily cheered by the small knot of enthusiasts present'. Mead, a Battersea lad, had been on the staff at The Oval but, according to the *Yorkshire Post*, 'Apparently he was not thought to have the qualities necessary for development into a first-class cricketer.' He might not have been the most attractive batsman to watch, one whose greatest skill was to be able to nudge almost any delivery into a gap in the field, but, in the whole history of county cricket, no man has matched the total of 48,892 runs that Mead went on to score for Hampshire.

It was late in the afternoon when he chipped a return catch to Hirst, and his departure allowed Yorkshire time to complete the victory. After two matches Hirst's wicket tally was already 13. 'He does not usually begin his wicket-taking so early in the season,' *The Times* observed.

In the next match he took another six against Cambridge University at Fenner's, but it was not a game that will have brought him any satisfaction. Putting out a full-strength side, Yorkshire fielded on the first day in what Lord Hawke – only a fortnight back from India – reckoned the coldest weather in which he had ever played cricket, and on the final day, after 'a terrific hailstorm' had swept across the ground in the early hours, they found themselves chasing 357 for victory. In a dramatic half hour they slumped from 36 for two to 51 all out. 'The feebleness of the opposition, and the extent of the defeat,' thundered the *Yorkshire Post*, 'were, to put it plainly, a humiliation upon Yorkshire cricket.' Then, running through the clatter of wickets with perfunctory brevity, it concluded, 'No useful purpose can be served by describing this debacle in detail.'

It was certainly no preparation for the first major contest of the summer, against Kent at the Private Banks Sports Ground in Catford.

The championship consisted of 16 counties, who were free to arrange their own fixtures, with a minimum of twelve games required for participation. As always Yorkshire arranged a full programme, their 28 games consisting of home and away fixtures against all the other counties except the 1905 newcomers Northamptonshire. By contrast, Middlesex were happy to play just 18, Nottinghamshire 20 and the rapidly improving Kent 22. There was a built-in inequality in the arrangements, and the winner was decided by a complex mathematical formula that subtracted defeats from victories and calculated the resulting number as a percentage of games won and lost. In theory, a county playing 12 matches and winning one, drawing 11, would finish with 100%, while one playing 28 matches and winning 27, losing one, would only have 93%. As became clear when the drama of that summer of 1906 unfolded, an unexpected defeat could have a catastrophic effect on a county's challenge for the championship.

The *Yorkshire Post* reckoned that the wickets at Catford did not have 'a reputation for durability', making it all the more surprising that the ground had come close to being selected as a Test match venue only three years earlier. On the Thursday morning, when the Yorkshire batsmen walked out to the middle, the weather was unpleasant. 'The district was shrouded in gloom, aggravated by the tall trees that surround the ground. The atmosphere was chilly, and topcoats were a necessity to all those who had to watch the cricket.' They went off for bad light for forty minutes before lunch and again in mid-afternoon.

They were not easy conditions for batting, and Kent had two of the finest bowlers in England: the tireless fast bowler Arthur Fielder and the guileful slow left-armer Colin Blythe. All eyes were on Yorkshire after their disgrace the previous day at Fenner's and, when Hirst came to the middle at 51 for three, *The Times* reported, 'To begin with, he found the bowling extremely difficult, and repeatedly was at fault in his timing of the ball.'

Gradually he found his touch and, when he drove Blythe to the mid-off boundary for his 17th four, he completed a century that one reporter reckoned was 'worth going miles to see'. At the other end Wilfred Rhodes had contributed seven to a partnership of 52, and the next man Charles Grimshaw was jeered by elements in the Catford crowd 'because he was parrying the bowling while Hirst was hitting it.' The *Yorkshire Post* deplored their ignorance, adding that 'in the South – with Lord's always an exception – local bias is too often accentuated by lack of knowledge of some of the essentials of the game.'

Hirst's hundred took his side to 199 for five, but next ball he 'snicked' an attempted cut to slip and Yorkshire ended the day on 229 all out. It was the first of his six hundreds that summer, and he scored it in a contest, the importance of which grew ever clearer as the race for the championship reached its epic climax in late August. As *Wisden* said of him at the end of that summer, 'When runs had to be made under trying conditions, he made them.'

The weather was bright and sunny on the second day, but the Catford pitch grew gradually more unpredictable. Both teams were dismissed in the day, and Kent – ending on 15 for no wicket – were left with a further 174 to make for victory.

"We won't score more than 140 on that pitch," the experienced Kent keeper Fred Huish said during the evening, and the following morning the batsmen – approaching their task with anxiety – were bowled out for 69.

To *The Times* correspondent, they made problems for themselves: 'Did they exaggerate the dangers of the various balls by investing them in imagination with additional terrors? Would not an eleven of cheerful, moderately good and delightfully ignorant batsmen have possibly done a little better?'

The honours of the morning went to George Hirst, who added seven wickets to the four he took in the first innings. 'A quiet winter seems to have done him good,' *The Times* observed, recalling his struggle with a troublesome leg in the latter stages of the previous summer. 'In his run to the wicket, there was all the old freedom both in the step and in the swing.'

Hirst's seven for 33 meant that the game was over in an hour and a quarter on the Saturday morning, but an even deadlier spell was to follow on Monday afternoon at Headingley. On a bitterly cold day – 'with a searching north-east wind more suggestive of football than cricket' – the visitors from Leicestershire fielded for most of the day as Yorkshire – thanks to a Denton hundred – made 244. Then in the closing hour 'they seemed unable to judge the bowling of Hirst and Rhodes' and were dismissed in 16.1 overs for 34. Hirst, 'in his most destructive mood', took seven for 13. He added five the next morning when Leicestershire followed on, and the match was all over by ten past one.

It was a disaster for Yorkshire County Cricket Club. With a total take of £49 – 11s, it was estimated that the home-and-away matches against the Midland county would result in a loss of £200, and once more there was talk that the county should give up on Leeds as a venue. Headingley was a private club, its subscription of one guinea entitling each member – accompanied by a lady – to attend the county cricket matches, with an additional five shillings buying access to the tennis courts or bowling green. The *Yorkshire Post*, sensing that the finer skills of cricket had not caught the imagination, suggested a radical alternative, one that perhaps anticipated the introduction of Twenty20 cricket almost a century later:

> We do not know if the Headingley authorities have thought of introducing baseball, which, because of the shortness of the innings, is found in America to be attractive, especially to those who want to go to a match where they can see all the players on both sides do something.

The rain that had never been far away during May followed the players to Birmingham for their next match. In a start-and-stop game that was washed away completely on the final day, 25 wickets fell for only 437 runs. Yet amid all this, on a damp pitch, George Hirst went in at 12 for three and was last man out for 104 in a total of 190. 'This he did without even making a bad stroke, and the hit that ended his innings was a good drive, which but for the high wind would probably have proved a six.'

The Times, noting that he was the only big run-scorer in county cricket to bat as low as five in the order, saw how well suited he was to the position:

> He can play two games. He can avoid a defeat or push home a victory. Best of all, he can combine both games with excellent judgment; and it is his temperament as much as his technical skill which enables him to do so.

In the first half of the following week Hirst was once more a bowler, he and Schofield Haigh taking 19 of the 20 Worcestershire wickets in a comfortable victory at the Amblecote ground outside Stourbridge. It was only the second time the home side had staged a match away from their scenic meadow in front of Worcester Cathedral, and the visitors – one of the principal supporters of Worcestershire's admission to the championship six years earlier – were not best pleased to be chosen to partake in this experiment. Though a healthy 4,000 crowd filled the ground on the first day, the *Yorkshire Post* correspondent thought that 'it was easy to see that not much knowledge of the finer points of cricket had been acquired in the neighbourhood.' Further, a shortage of suitable accommodation forced the Yorkshire side to travel into Birmingham each night.

A damp May ended with a trip to the New College ground in Oxford, where George Hirst – ensuring no repetition of the debacle in Cambridge – rounded off his month's work with an innings of 169. He was the leading wicket-taker in England, and this was his third hundred of the summer. 'Hirst,' *The Times* wrote, 'has by his fine all-round play contradicted the common contention that a man cannot bowl much and bowl fast and make a large number of runs as well.'

Yorkshire's bowling attack that summer was dominated by three men: George Hirst, Wilfred Rhodes and Schofield Haigh. They had all served together under Lord Hawke through the previous eight summers when five championships had been won, and in 1906 they took more than 80% of the county's wickets.

Rhodes as a man was the antithesis of Hirst, dour and unsmiling, a crafty cricketer where Hirst was more of a natural, but Haigh was another, like Hirst, with an infectious smile. 'One of the best-tempered, happy souls I've ever come across,' Lord Hawke called him, though sometimes 'He grew a little down on his luck and needed bucking up. He could send down a very fast yorker but was lazy about doing so. But if I chipped in with "Now, Schofie, time for that yorker!", then out it would come, and very likely the middle stump too.'

Haigh and Hirst were kindred spirits, the same age and with the same love of a joke. Playing at a new ground, they say, Haigh arrived just ahead of Hirst and took the gateman quietly to one side: "Don't look now," he said, "but there's a man been following me. Thinks he's George Hirst.

Whatever you do, don't let him in." Barred from entry moments later, Hirst stood patiently. "All right," he said. "If I'm not George Hirst, I'm not. But you'd better go and tell his Lordship that he'll be a man short." Later in the year, when Haigh was out of the team injured, Hirst got his own back, getting a burly waiter in the lunch tent at Chesterfield to throw Haigh out as an uninvited intruder.

In that last week of May 1906, at Stourbridge and at Oxford, Schofield Haigh took 20 wickets, putting him to the top of the national bowling averages. With Billy Ringrose unfit since the match at Fenner's, Yorkshire were for the most part a three-man attack that summer, but such was their dominance and the stamina of that trio – Hirst, Haigh and Rhodes, all men from the Huddersfield area – that they often had no need of a fourth.

GEORGE HIRST IN MAY

Date	Opponents	Venue	Batting 1	Batting 2	Bowling Overs	W-R	Overs	W-R
7-9	MCC	Lord's	61	34	13	2-47	18	2-52
10-12	Hampshire	Southampton	41	4*	27	6-87	26	3-62
14-16	Cambridge U	Fenner's	30	0	18.1	2-54	18	4-51
17-19	Kent	Catford	101	4	19.3	4-46	18.4	7-33
21-23	Leics	Headingley	3		8.1	7-18	16	5-48
24-26	Warwicks	Edgbaston	104		18	2-38	16	1-18
28-30	Worcs	Stourbridge	4		28.5	6-70	25	3-59
31-2	Oxford U	Oxford	169		9	1-12	11	2-15

BATTING

M	Inns	NO	HS	Runs	Average	100	50
8	12	1	169	555	50.45	3	1

BOWLING

Overs	Mdns	Runs	Wkts	Average	10wm	5wi
290.2	83	710	57	12.45	2	5

CHAMPIONSHIP TABLE – 2 JUNE

	Played	Won	Drawn	Lost	Points	Percentage
Surrey	8	5	3	0	5	100.00
Lancashire	5	4	1	0	4	100.00
Yorkshire	5	4	1	0	4	100.00
Essex	4	2	2	0	2	100.00
Somerset	2	1	1	0	1	100.00
Nottinghamshire	4	2	1	1	1	33.33
Middlesex	2	1	0	1	0	0.00
Sussex	3	1	1	1	0	0.00
Gloucestershire	3	1	1	1	0	0.00
Warwickshire	4	1	1	2	-1	-33.33
Northamptonshire	4	1	0	3	-2	-50.00
Leicestershire	5	1	0	4	-3	-60.00
Kent	2	0	1	1	-1	-100.00
Worcestershire	3	0	1	2	-2	-100.00
Derbyshire	4	0	0	4	-4	-100.00
Hampshire	4	0	0	4	-4	-100.00

The Month of June

There were no Test matches in the summer of 1906. The visiting tourists were the West Indians, playing a round of county matches but still 22 years away from elevation to Test status.

So the county championship took centre stage all summer, and what a championship it turned out to be! At the end of May there were five unbeaten sides, and the Whitsuntide Bank Holiday pitted two of them against each other in the traditional Roses match.

Despite weekend rain, 18,000 spectators crowded into the Park Avenue ground at Bradford, and they watched with anticipation as Lancashire's captain Archie MacLaren opted to bat first on the soft pitch. Park Avenue had already acquired a reputation as a ground that provided encouragement to the bowler, and so it proved that morning.

'No one man, however eminent, can make a cricket team,' declared the *Yorkshire Post* the following morning. 'Yet in its essentials yesterday was a Hirst day.'

He bowled, according to *The Times*, 'at a great pace and with an awkward swerve' and soon removed MacLaren. 'From the first over,' the *Post* reckoned, 'it was easy for the practised eye to see that Hirst was in his dangerous or, as he himself has described it, his funny mood.'

Rhodes, taking the new ball, was less successful but, once Haigh took over, wickets started to fall. 35 for one became 40 for four. Then, with lunch approaching, Hirst – who had bowled unchanged through the morning – sent Lancashire tumbling from 51 for four to 56 for nine, leaving the field with figures of six for 16. Then, with Lancashire all out for 67, the man of the summer underlined that the pitch could be batted upon, scoring a battling 58 and taking Yorkshire into a lead that would go on to give them a six-wicket victory at half past four the next afternoon. The second-day crowd of 22,000 raised the takings for the match to almost £1,500. 'These figures,' the *Yorkshire Post* said, 'are an effective answer to those critics who have taken advantage of unseasonable weather to cry "stinking fish" about the game of cricket.'

There were now only three unbeaten counties – Yorkshire, Surrey and the unfancied Essex. In the view of *The Times*, 'Yorkshire, in spite of their two unexpected defeats in games outside the championship competition, are unmistakably the best all-round county eleven of the summer' and 'Hirst is essentially the greatest cricketer of the season, and the side for which he plays is usually the side one expects to win.'

June 1906. Women stepped up their campaign to win the vote with a mass deputation to the Prime Minister. Trade unionists demanded a 48-hour working week, and a workman from Staines, his family in the workhouse, started a ten-week, 513-mile walk in search of work that ended in late

August when he gave himself up, still unemployed, to Chesterfield police.

Across Europe the threat of revolution spread. In Madrid 18 people were killed when a bomb was hurled at the King and Queen of Spain, in Rome a plot to kill the King of Italy was uncovered, and in Russia – in the words of *The Times* – 'the police were organising massacres of the Jews, thus attempting to divert the revolutionary movement.' Meanwhile the *Yorkshire Post*, joining the general alarm, found significant anarchist centres not only in Leeds but in Hull where revolutionary literature was coming in through the port.

County cricket was a happy escape from all this, and George Hirst's all-round summer of glory continued at Chesterfield where he 'again bowled heroically', sending down 27 overs in each innings, taking nine wickets and hitting a second innings fifty that 'came to the rescue' when Derbyshire, of all counties, looked set to pull off an unexpected victory.

A comfortable win followed against Hampshire at Sheffield, then another against Middlesex at Lord's, where there was no repeat of the near-calamity of the previous summer. Ronnie Ashton recalls how George used to tell of that match.

> We were left to get 100 to win and, when we reached 50 or so for no wicket, Lord Hawke said to me, 'Look, George, if I leave you here with a couple of others, I'll get the rest of the team off and we can catch an earlier train.' 'Oh righto, my Lord,' I said. And before I knew where I was, we'd lost three wickets, and I was going out to bat, the last man in. The first ball I got landed on my big toe.

He survived, guiding his side to victory, and they caught a cab to the station.

> And bless my soul, the first person we met there was Lord Hawke, walking up and down the platform. They'd missed the train. 'By Jove, my Lord,' I said. 'You're not to do that again.'

Hirst knew his place, but he was also happy in a quiet, firm way to speak his mind.

From Lord's in 1906 they travelled back to Bradford where they beat Essex and, in so doing, effectively ended the East London club's involvement in the championship race. *The Times*, noting how close to financial ruin Essex had been two years previously, thought that the ever-growing emphasis on the competition did have some 'undesirable' consequences: 'A county side may play good and sportsmanlike cricket for four months, but in most cases practical public support is withdrawn directly that side no longer seems to have a chance of gaining the championship.' It argued that the decision whether the competition should be continued be given 'special consideration'.

Wisden the following year also expressed some unease about the rising importance of the county championship. 'It is a means to an end and not an end in itself. Its existence has been justified, I think, by the immense growth of county cricket in the last twenty years or so, but it must not be made into a fetish. If it were abolished tomorrow the game of cricket would go on just as before, and we should find something to put in its place.'

At Bradford Essex began their first innings on the second morning in dramatic circumstances. JWHT Douglas, the future England captain, took strike and, with the very first ball, Hirst sent down a full toss that 'swung in from quite a yard on the off side of the wicket and fell upon the off stump.' Two balls later the prolific Percy Perrin was bowled by a similar delivery, and in no time the scoreboard read 26 for eight. They were all out twice in the day, with Hirst's swerve again dismissing Douglas for a duck.

Yorkshire had played ten matches in the championship and won nine of them, all bar the one at Edgbaston where rain had rescued Warwickshire. Meanwhile their most likely rivals, Surrey, had lost their unbeaten record in an epic contest at The Oval, notable above all else for the emergence of Frank Woolley.

The son of a motor-car mechanic, the 19-year-old Woolley – who was deputising for the injured Colin Blythe – was playing only his third game for Kent, 'almost trembling' – in his own words – as he stepped out onto the great Oval field. Yet, opening the bowling with Arthur Fielder, the pair of them soon had the home team six wickets down, and it was at this point, he later wrote, that he asked his bowling partner about Tom Hayward, the Surrey batsman whose runs that summer were breaking all the records. 'I had never seen him, but I had heard of his habit of going in to bat at twelve o'clock and pushing the ball about at will until he'd had enough. "When's Tom Hayward coming in?" I asked, almost in a whisper. "Tom?" came the reply. "Why, you bowled him second ball!"

With 72 out of 200 in the Kent first innings and eight wickets in the match, Woolley had done much to put his side in a winning position, and they only wanted 128 for victory. Yet how far away that total must have seemed when he found himself in the middle with Arthur Fielder, the last men in and still another 19 runs required! He tried to keep strike, and fortune shone on them when, with ten to win, Fielder pushed a ball into the covers and set off for an impossible single. The throw went wide, it ran for four overthrows, and suddenly there were just five to win.

Lord Dalmeny, the Surrey captain, moved his fielders all around the young batsman. A 'crows-round-a-bone field,' Woolley called it and, after leaving a wide delivery, he crashed a four in the air through the covers. 'Even then he looked an England player,' the Surrey keeper Herbert

Strudwick wrote. 'We were all very much taken with him and wished he was on our side.'

Scores were level, and there must have been some in the crowd who thought that they might witness a repeat of the previous year's tie. And so it nearly proved when a great appeal for lbw echoed around the ground. But Woolley survived and, chancing his arm once more, flashed hard and watched as the resulting edge flew over the slips for another four.

The crowd swarmed on. A spectator grabbed Woolley's bat, he received 'two proper whacks' on the shoulders from an umbrella, and in the mayhem two sovereigns were pressed into his hand. 'At the finish,' he wrote, 'probably in my hurry to escape, I actually got into my bath with one boot on.'

Kent were a county busy training its own cricketers in its Tonbridge nursery. They had a young side, full of promise, and this victory over the mighty Surrey added fresh excitement to what was already proving a vintage county summer. To Yorkshire, at this stage, it seemed a beneficial result, as the table on 21 June showed:

	Played	*Won*	*Drawn*	*Lost*	*Points*	*Percentage*
Yorkshire	10	9	1	0	9	100.00
Surrey	13	9	3	1	8	80.00
Lancashire	10	7	2	1	6	75.00
Nottinghamshire	9	4	3	2	2	33.33
Kent	7	4	1	2	2	33.33

From this point, only defeats could knock Yorkshire off the top of the table. At Trent Bridge they might have lost to Nottinghamshire, but David Denton saved them, becoming the first batsman ever to hit a century in each innings for Yorkshire.

Then came Kent to Bramall Lane, Sheffield, and they gained a first innings lead, thanks to a brilliant century by the amateur Kenneth Hutchings.

George Hirst was a specialist mid-off fielder, in an era when the classical batting style was to play off the front foot and to drive the ball hard in the direction of mid-off. 'He was like a sandbank,' wrote Pelham Warner – or, as a Kirkheaton friend of Hirst once said, 'You'd as soon get a ball through a brick wall as past him at mid-off.' But Hutchings, according to one contemporary observer, 'drives the ball with a vigour that even GL Jessop cannot emulate.' 'The hardest driver I ever saw,' Woolley wrote many years later. 'His off-drive became as near the shot-out-of-a-gun as a ball hit by a bat could ever approach in speed.' Denton, fielding on the boundary that day at Sheffield, complained that his hands were stung as if he were fielding at cover point. 'Mr Hutchings,' Woolley wrote, almost as the ultimate tribute, 'was the only batsman who could make George Hirst retreat at mid-off.'

By close of play on the second day. Yorkshire, on 124 for six, had a lead of just 119, and it looked as if Kent would inflict defeat on them just as they had done on Surrey earlier in the month.

But George Hirst was not out, and on the final day he gave 'a masterly performance', at first batting with 'admirable defensiveness', then – when the lead had reached comfortable proportions – making 'every kind of stroke' and, as the *Yorkshire Post* put it, 'there is no stroke that Hirst cannot make with confidence.' By close of play it was Kent, with seven wickets down, who were hanging on to the draw.

That innings took Hirst past 1,000 runs, and the next day at Leyton, Thursday 28 June, in a 28-over spell, he added his 99th and 100th wickets, the first man in England to 100.

In 1875 WG Grace had completed the double on 26 July, and George Hirst himself had broken that record in 1901 when he brought up the double a full fortnight faster, on 12 July. Now he had taken another fortnight off his own record, and nobody in a hundred years since then has equalled even his earlier record.

Just as the previous summer at Leyton, when Yorkshire played out the last day for the draw that guaranteed them the championship, they had the worse of the contest and again they found themselves playing for the draw on the last day, this time Rhodes, Tunnicliffe and Hirst the object of the frustrated crowd's wrath. 'A section of the 10,000 spectators,' the *Yorkshire Post* reported, 'betrayed an unmannerly and unsportsmanlike disposition to jeer the Yorkshiremen when they were batting to save the game.' It clearly got under the skin of the correspondent, as his next sentence revealed:

> There is no crowd in any first-class cricket ground in England more ignorant, or at any rate more successful in concealing their knowledge of the ethics of cricket, than the Leyton public and their evidence of intelligence does not increase from year to year.

The Times blamed Essex for declaring their innings too late on the final day, adding that 'Hirst's pulling was the one interesting thing in the spiritless afternoon's cricket.'

The end of June had been reached, and Yorkshire remained unbeaten. In 16 matches in just eight weeks George Hirst had batted 27 times, sent down 639 overs and completed the fastest double in the history of cricket.

GEORGE HIRST IN JUNE

Date	Opponents	Venue	Batting 1	Batting 2	Bowling Overs	Bowling W-R	Bowling Overs	Bowling W-R
4-6	Lancashire	Bradford	58	5*	21	6-20	21.1	2-44
7-9	Derbyshire	Chesterfield	1	53	27	5-80	27	4-63
11-13	Hampshire	Sheffield	67	15	15	2-41	20	2-59
14-16	Middlesex	Lord's	41	16	16	0-29	17	0-16
18-20	Essex	Bradford	33		12.2	5-32	19	4-66
21-23	Notts	Trent Bridge	24	76	29	2-95	10	1-27
25-27	Kent	Sheffield	4	93	34	5-94	21	3-61
28-30	Essex	Leyton	15	57*	28	2-75	31	4-78

BATTING IN JUNE

M	*Inns*	*NO*	*HS*	*Runs*	*Average*	*100*	*50*
8	15	2	93	558	42.92	–	6

BATTING IN MAY & JUNE

M	*Inns*	*NO*	*HS*	*Runs*	*Average*	*100*	*50*
16	27	3	169	1113	46.37	3	7

BOWLING IN JUNE

Overs	*Mdns*	*Runs*	*Wkts*	*Average*	*10wm*	*5wi*
348.3	77	880	47	18.72	–	4

BOWLING IN MAY & JUNE

Overs	*Mdns*	*Runs*	*Wkts*	*Average*	*10wm*	*5wi*
638.5	160	1590	104	15.28	2	9

CHAMPIONSHIP TABLE – 30 JUNE

	Played	*Won*	*Drawn*	*Lost*	*Points*	*Percentage*
Yorkshire	13	9	4	0	9	100.00
Surrey	13	9	3	1	8	80.00
Lancashire	12	8	2	2	6	60.00
Nottinghamshire	11	5	4	2	3	42.85
Kent	10	5	3	2	3	42.85
Essex	10	4	4	2	2	33.33
Warwickshire	10	4	4	2	2	33.33
Somerset	7	2	2	3	-1	-20.00
Sussex	7	2	2	3	-1	-20.00
Worcestershire	6	1	3	2	-1	-33.33
Middlesex	7	2	1	4	-2	-33.33
Northamptonshire	9	2	1	6	-4	-50.00
Gloucestershire	7	1	2	4	-3	-60.00
Leicestershire	12	2	1	9	-7	-63.63
Hampshire	10	1	2	7	-6	-75.00
Derbyshire	10	1	0	9	-8	-80.00

George Hirst the man

George Hirst married Emma Kilner on New Year's Day 1896, and they set up home in Field Place, Kirkheaton, where their three children were born: Jim in 1896, Anne in 1899 and Molly on 29 April 1906, days before the start of his golden summer. "It adds another dimension to his achievement, doesn't it?" Molly's daughter Lindsay says. "Whenever he came home for the night, there would have been a baby crying."

The family moved to 33 Glebe Street in Marsh, Huddersfield, a terraced house, when Molly was still small. Leaving Kirkheaton gave the children a chance of a better education than George had had. Jim walked each day to Almondbury Grammar School; Anne and Molly attended Greenhead High where, as daughters of the great cricketer, they were accepted on reduced fees.

At home George Hirst was a quiet man, rarely raising his voice – though Ruth remembers her father Jim's story of the night when, as a young man, he crept in late. "His bedroom was in the attic, above his father's, and he started to take his shoes off. Without thinking he dropped the first one with a great clonk. Then he suddenly remembered, and he took the second one off ever so quietly. A few minutes later, this voice came up from below: 'For God's sake, Jim, drop the other one so I can get back to sleep.'"

Most of the time George was happy to sit with his pipe and to leave the talking to his wife Emma.

"Granny was the one with the stories," Jim's daughter Margaret remembers. "She would chat, and he would just go behind his newspaper. One story I remember her telling us was about the day when my father was a little baby and George the Fifth and Queen Mary, when they were the Duke and Duchess of York, came to visit Kirkheaton. Granny sat my father on the wall, waiting for the carriage to come by, and standing next to them was an old local man with his head on the wall. The Duke was much smaller than the Duchess and, when they came by, and the Duchess was sitting upright, waving graciously, with the little Duke beside her, this old boy turned to Granny. 'By gum, missus,' he said. 'I bet she makes him turn the mangle.'"

Jim had two daughters, Margaret and Ruth, born in 1924 and 1927. Anne remained unmarried, caring for her parents in their old age. And Molly married a Dundee jute merchant and moved to Scotland, where she had one daughter, Lindsay, born in 1944.

"My mother revered my grandfather," Lindsay says. "All his children did. I've never heard a word of criticism about him. I grew up on stories about him. And that year of 1906 was like a beacon year in all our lives. I've still got a pair of inscribed silver candlesticks that Lord Hawke gave him in honour of his achievement."

Her own memories are limited. She came down from Scotland to stay with her grandparents occasionally, and she remembers him as "a grandfather who spoiled me." She also retains a letter he wrote to her when she had just started at school and was being bullied by the other children, a letter that he accompanied with a photograph of himself walking down the street.

> My dear Lindsay
> I was so pleased to get that nice card on my birthday. I am sending you a photo of an old man who is very fond of you. I hope that you are liking school more now. Do your lessons and stick up for yourself, and all will come right in the end.
> Love to Mam and Dad and your dear self
> From Grandad

The values of the old man ran down the generations of the family. "He was always very unassuming, and that came down to me. Always be courteous and respectful to others, whatever their station in life. Be cheerful, good-humoured, never criticise others, never boast. Have self-control, self-discipline. They might not be fashionable ideas today, but they were good values. He was a man with great strength of character. And he always tried to see the best in other people."

George Hirst had left school at the age of ten, and he had graduated in his late teens from the world of looms and dyes in Kirkheaton to a cricket environment in which he played alongside the Honourable Stanley Jackson, son of a baron who had prospered in the Industrial Revolution, and Lord Hawke, whose ancestor had been an admiral and had defeated the French fleet half a century before Nelson.

He had grown up speaking the broad dialect of the West Riding. Hawke wrote of the evening when they had a competition to see who could tell 'the best Yorkshire tale in genuine lingo without breaking out of the dialect.' A silver tobacco box was the prize, and 'Georgie Hirst won it easy with 90 per cent marks.'

Yet Hirst was determined to better himself and, according to Lindsay, "At home he always spoke the Queen's English." He was not a tyrannical husband and father, but he did have standards that he liked to uphold. "He had a thing about not wasting electricity. He was always turning the lights off. He hated women smoking, and he couldn't bear swearing."

Apart from being a great sportsman, he also had a fine singing voice. 'When he sang,' the Leicester batsman AE Knight wrote, 'he sang in voice of gentlest tenor, the quaint old homely songs which you can only hear in country inns, remote from towns.'

"In one of the presentations they gave him a piano," grand-daughter Margaret says. "I can see him playing and singing. 'Oh those golden slippers, eh those golden slippers.' He could play the piano – but only oompah-pah."

"My mother would accompany him," Lindsay recalls. "And he'd sing songs like *I'll Sing Thee Songs of Araby* and *Thora*."

I'll sing thee songs of Araby,
And tales of fair Kashmir,
Wild tales to cheat thee of a sigh,
Or charm thee to a tear.

"I remember, when he was an old man, he used to sing *We'll Gather Lilacs*."

And in the evening by the firelight glow,
You'll hold me close and never let me go,
Your eyes will tell me all I want to know,
When you come home once more.

The Month of July

July began with Yorkshire's second visit to Headingley, and the weather was even more unkind than it had been for their first in May. Monday was washed out, and on Tuesday, when Yorkshire battled to 232 all out against Gloucestershire, there was a foggy, murky air. The *Yorkshire Post*, keeping up to date with the latest technology, said that 'electric lights had to be turned on in shop and counting house.'

For this match Yorkshire called up a new fast bowler: Cecil Parkin, a 20-year-old professional at the Ossett club. Before the match he admitted to Lord Hawke that he was born just beyond the boundary in Eaglescliffe, County Durham. Hawke's reply – "We're not particular about a few yards" – overcame the problem but, alas, it was overruled by MCC after the match and Parkin, later of Lancashire and England, had only one Yorkshire appearance to look back on when he wrote his memoirs.

> My short life in the Yorkshire eleven was sufficient for me to discover what a great-hearted man George Hirst is. When I went on to bowl, I had a severe attack of nerves; of course I was then only a nipper. And just as I was rolling up my sleeves and my fingers were trembling on the ball, I felt a pat on the back. It was George Hirst who, realising that I needed a friendly word, came forward to cheer me up. "Don't worry but stick at it," he said; and I shall never forget his kindly glance. He is a human being in a thousand is Hirst, one of nature's gentlemen – not only a great cricketer, but, more important, a great man.

Parkin took two wickets as Gloucestershire were all out for 151. Yorkshire hit some quick runs and declared, but time ran out with the visitors, six wickets down, hanging on for a draw. The West Countrymen were struggling that summer, bottom of the table by the end of July, and few will have anticipated that, in the return match at Bristol in late August, in the match that would settle the destination of the championship, they would put up the fight that they did. But then Gloucestershire was not like Yorkshire, not a regular side who played all summer together. They were full of amateurs who dropped in and out of the team, wanted to play during their holidays in August, perhaps did not fancy a trip to Leeds. There were eight of them in the side when they played Yorkshire at Bristol, and only two of these had played at Headingley. With the likes of Charles Townsend, Cyril Sewell and Gilbert Jessop among them, they were always going to be more formidable in Bristol in August.

But that was still to come.

Yorkshire, unbeaten at the halfway point in their programme, headed for Dewsbury's Savile Town ground in the local Feast Week, to play

Nottinghamshire. It was a large ground, bigger in playing area than Bradford Park Avenue, with a good batting surface, but somehow things never seemed to go smoothly there. In the previous eight years only once had the match lasted a full three days, and in that time one game had had to be suspended when the players were attacked by swarms of greenfly and in another the Derbyshire team had had to field in their ordinary clothes when they discovered that a burst pipe had flooded their dressing room overnight.

With the first seven balls of the match against Nottinghamshire George Hirst took three wickets. He took the first seven in all, and Yorkshire were batting before lunch. But he only made 14, the Yorkshire first innings lead was only 77 and by close of play the Notts openers had knocked off 75 of them. A day that had begun in triumph for Yorkshire ended, in the words of *The Times*, with 'the visitors on terms with their opponents again'.

Heavy rain fell in the night, and George Hirst took another seven wickets as the visitors collapsed from 135 for one to 170 all out. That left Yorkshire with just 94 for victory, but wickets quickly fell and Hirst was back in action at 21 for three. That summer the great all-rounder from Kirkheaton had come to the rescue every time his side had been in peril but, as the *Yorkshire Post* reflected, 'One man cannot always be relied upon to win a match.' He was caught by the wicket-keeper for four, and in no time the score was 26 for eight. The last three in the order, led by Schofield Haigh, engaged in some 'spirited hitting' but it was to no avail. At half past four Yorkshire were all out 26 runs short of victory.

The game was over. There would be no play for the Feast Week holiday-makers to enjoy on the Saturday. 'Dewsbury folk,' the *Yorkshire Post* wrote, 'are still asking when fortune will favour them with three days' county cricket.'

Yorkshire had lost for the first time in twelve months, for the first time in ten years to Nottinghamshire. Though the dramatic outcome merited only a few lines in *The Times*, whose attention was all on the Oxford-Cambridge and Eton-Winchester contests, the *Yorkshire Post* reported that the news of Yorkshire's defeat was greeted in the Old Trafford pavilion with 'a huge howl of rejoicing' and 'a succession of cheers'. It was not behaviour that impressed the *Post*: 'Most sportsmen will regret to see a feeling of this kind exhibited, for it suggests a spirit of envy and uncharitableness that is not at all creditable to the game.'

That evening Lancashire completed an innings victory over Gloucestershire, and – under the complicated mathematical formula employed – Yorkshire's single defeat suddenly gave the championship table a very different look:

	Played	Won	Drawn	Lost	Points	Percentage
Surrey	15	11	3	1	10	83.33
Yorkshire	15	9	5	1	8	80.00
Lancashire	14	9	3	2	7	63.63
Nottinghamshire	13	6	5	2	4	50.00
Kent	11	5	4	2	3	42.85

July 1906. The All-England Lawn Tennis Championships attracted record crowds of 6,000 to Worple Road in Wimbledon. The holder of the Men's Singles, Laurie Doherty, retained his title – though, by the rules of the time, he was only required to play one match, against Frank Riseley who had defeated Arthur Gore in the final of the All-Comers' Competition. All three men were English, occasioning the writer Alfred Gibson of the *Morning Leader* to declare triumphantly, 'The Americans and Australians have long since been weeded out. This is rather curious, when one remembers that a well-known authority has declared that "Englishmen cannot play lawn tennis." According to the same authority, they cannot even hold their rackets properly. But they beat the world all the same.'

Yet lawn tennis was not considered to be one of the manly sports. 'When any of my boys became a happy father,' Lord Hawke wrote, 'the question always was: "What's the kid – a lawn-tenniser or a cricketer?", that being the way of finding out whether it was a girl or a boy.'

These were still the infant days of most sports. Two years earlier Riseley had reached the final of the All-Comers when, locked at two sets all with his opponent, they had retired exhausted and agreed to toss a coin. The Olympic Games of that year was a little-supported venture in St Louis, Missouri, in which the American marathon winner was disqualified for taking a lift in a lorry while the eventual British winner came home thanks to doses of strychnine and brandy en route. There were only a small number of women's events, notably archery, though in the summer of 1906, when a woman parachutist fell to her death in West Yorkshire, a bill was introduced into the House of Commons, proposing the banning of ladies from all dangerous sports.

Meanwhile, in Paris, 'a new malady' was discovered: 'telephonitis', with the victims all female operators. They were thought to be suffering from 'the constant contact with electric currents', and the French authorities 'resolved to replace them with men'.

July 1906. The newspapers were full of advertisements for medicines. Beecham's Pills – "Will keep you prime". Phosferine – "The greatest of all tonics." Owbridge's Lung Tonic – "An absolute necessity to everybody."

"My grandfather wasn't a drinker really," Margaret Ashton says of George Hirst. "But, when he was really tired at the tea interval, he would have a nip of gin and sherry mixed. That helped him through."

He must have been tired by the second week of July. Yorkshire did not have a fixture in the first half of the week, but Hirst was invited to Lord's – with David Denton, Wilfred Rhodes and Schofield Haigh – to represent the Players against the Gentlemen. Hirst, however, did not play. According to *Wisden*, 'he felt obliged to save himself for Yorkshire matches,' a decision that evoked criticism from many at Lord's. In his place John Gunn of Nottinghamshire took the new ball for the Players, and his wicketless spell allowed Arthur Fielder at the other end to become the only man in the history of the Lord's fixture to take all ten wickets in an innings. Would he have done it with Hirst at the other end? And, back in Huddersfield, would Hirst – for all his kindliness – have had the same passing thought that the great Sydney Barnes had after watching Jim Laker's historic triumph over the Australians: "No beggar got all ten when I was bowling at the other end."

Refreshed by his break, Hirst hit a hundred in a victory over Sussex at Hove. Some indication of his summer's labours can be gleaned from the comment in the *Yorkshire Post* after his 26 overs on the first day: 'The impression was conveyed on an easy paced wicket, with Hirst and Haigh feeling the effects of this heavy but brilliant season's work, that another fast bowler is essential to the team.' Then, in Sussex's second innings, Hirst 'stepped into one of the bowler's footmarks and so wrenched his left leg that soon afterwards he had to relinquish the attack. Though later on he tested the limb again, he could only bowl one over.'

It was an alarm but not it seems a great one. The following week, at Sheffield and Huddersfield, he bowled 61 overs, as well as making a vital 89 in the first of the two matches. Lord Hawke was absent, off playing a week of country house cricket at Woolverstone Park in Ipswich, home of his fellow Old Etonian John Berners. In his absence his Yorkshire team won both their games but, on his return, there was a scare at Bradford when they were eight second innings wickets down against Sussex and only 35 runs ahead. It was still the morning of the final day, and Hirst had just been dismissed, unluckily dragging a ball onto his stumps, for 42: 'worth 100 in less critical circumstances,' the *Yorkshire Post* reckoned. It left only Hawke and his keeper David Hunter, the two 'old dogs' of the team, to be followed by George Deyes, a relative newcomer playing in place of the injured Schofield Haigh and one whose batting the next summer – when he made three runs in his first 14 innings – was bad enough to win him entry in one statistical compendium for the worst run of batting of all time.

Hawke and Hunter. One had learnt his cricket at Eton, the other on the sands at Scarborough. One, a lover of shooting, had given Yorkshire cricket a discipline and a seriousness that would stand it in good stead for decades to come. The other, a bell-ringer and breeder of canaries, was known to think that county cricket had become too serious. Yet they loved to bat together in a crisis and, with an improbable contribution of eight from Deyes, they left Sussex 123 to win in just under two hours. It was a task that the visitors gave up, once George Hirst had removed three of their batsmen before the total had reached double figures.

It was a great escape for Yorkshire, and they travelled to The Oval in good spirits for a game that looked like being the championship showdown.

From Bradford to London was a gruelling train journey. They left on the 6.03 train, changed at Masbrough at 7.42, again at Leicester where they had a half-hour wait, and they arrived at St Pancras at 11.15. It was gone midnight when they reached their rooms, but at least they were spared the strain of fielding first on what turned out to be 'a hot and tiring day'. Twenty-seven thousand spectators packed the ground, including the Prince and Princess of Wales and their children, and they were disappointed when the Surrey captain Lord Dalmeny lost the toss and they were deprived of the opportunity to watch their premier trio of batsmen – Hayward, Hayes and the young Jack Hobbs – pile up the runs. Instead, Yorkshire – whose strength, according to *The Times*, lay in their 'recuperative power when in difficulties' – struggled against the lively bowling of Walter Lees and particularly the young Neville Knox, thought by many to be the fastest bowler in England at this time. Five wickets went down for 49, including that of George Hirst for his first duck since the disgrace at Fenner's in early May. 'His dismissal was very disappointing,' *The Times* thought. 'He is a master of the pull stroke, but he endeavoured to put it in force before he had given himself time to get the pace of the wicket.'

Bill Bowes recalls talking to Hirst about his favourite pull, whether it was a shot that carried too much risk. "Of course, I used to get out occasionally when I played it," he said. "But by and large it was well worth it. It got hundreds of runs for Yorkshire."

For Yorkshire, note. Not for GH Hirst.

At The Oval Yorkshire recovered to 186 all out, but that was soon to look a poor score when the Surrey batsmen got to work under the quieter sun of the evening. They closed on 135 for one and went on next day to 387. By the time George Hirst came to the wicket on the final morning, Yorkshire were 145 for four, still 56 runs away from saving the innings defeat. At the other end was the Honourable FS Jackson, the England captain who had retired the previous August and who was making his first appearance of the summer for Yorkshire. 'All depended on these two men, and they seemed to realise their responsibilities.'

Then Jackson reached for a wide ball from Knox and was caught and, when Taylor and Wilkinson quickly followed, there were seven wickets down and Yorkshire were still nine runs in arrears. Haigh offered spirited resistance, but he fell to the last ball before lunch, when Yorkshire were 40 ahead with only Lord Hawke and the injured Rothery to come.

Wisden reckoned Hirst's innings at The Oval that day one of his two greatest in a summer in which his runs flowed with regularity. He defended with determination, he took 'three nasty blows' on the body from Knox and, according to *The Times*, 'several times he made the particular pull of which he is a master in regard of balls which, if he had missed them, must in all probability have struck him in the face.'

'Hirst it was who received the greatest share of the bowlers' attentions,' the *Yorkshire Post* reported, and the *Daily Telegraph*, describing several blows he took from the fast bowlers, referred to 'a delay of two or three minutes' when he 'received a stinging blow just above the wrist' and a second, longer one when 'a ball took the skin off one of his knuckles.' This was a hard, bouncy wicket, unlike so many that Yorkshire had played on that summer, and the Surrey bowlers, especially Knox, were the better suited to it. Herbert Strudwick the Surrey keeper wrote of the game, 'I can hear now Lord Dalmeny saying, every time the ball flew past the batsman's head, "Well bowled, Neville!" Hirst must have been black and blue after that match.'

At one stage, Hirst made only one scoring shot in 50 minutes. 'Yet,' in the words of the *Yorkshire Post*, 'he defied all the "bumping" for three and a quarter hours.'

The ground was packed. There were 'well over 80,000 attending over the three days', and at this stage of the Saturday afternoon 'the Surrey crowd, that curious combination of flamboyant enthusiasm, ignorance and goodwill began to feel uneasy as to whether there would be time to permit of their side scoring the runs they would require to win.'

Hawke stayed for 70 minutes for eight runs – 'the noble Lord's eight not being estimated by numerical value' – then Hirst was bowled by Lees by a ball which 'turned quickly and gave him little chance of stopping it.'

His 87, *The Times* judged, 'in the circumstances and the physical conditions which existed, may be regarded as one of the greatest innings he has ever played for Yorkshire.'

'No one,' said the *Daily Telegraph*, 'could have tried harder to save a lost game or played with greater pluck.'

Surrey needed 97 runs for victory, and they lost only Jack Hobbs in getting them, the main focus of attention in the latter stages being on what *The Times* referred to as 'the Saturday afternoon element' of the crowd. They encroached repeatedly onto the outfield, and in the end 'the few attendants and half-dozen policemen who remonstrated with them had to leave them masters of the situation.' When scores were brought level with a four, this 'disorderly section' surged onto the field, as far as the wickets, and such was the unmanageable turmoil that ensued that the only way the game could be completed was for Schofield Haigh to send down 'an intentional wide'.

In the championship table Surrey, with just the one defeat – by one wicket to Kent – moved up to 86.66% while Yorkshire fell back to 71.42. 'Yorkshire have still more than a good chance of keeping their honours,' *The Times* thought, 'and Kent, who play Surrey next at Blackheath, may in the end do better than either Yorkshire or Surrey.'

The month of July ended with Yorkshire at Hull, bowling out Worcestershire for 25 and winning by an innings. Hirst had match figures of eight for 60, but the headlines went to Herbert Sedgwick, a professional from the Littleborough club who had reported to Hull 'for a net to demonstrate his bowling abilities'. At this point Lord Hawke became unavailable with an attack of lumbago, a complaint that would keep him out of the remaining championship matches, and Sedgwick found himself not only playing but opening the bowling. With an effective use of away swing, he took five wickets for eight runs in the Worcester first innings and a hat-trick in the second. 'An extraordinary success,' the *Yorkshire Post* called it, 'though he may find it difficult to live up to.'

The *Yorkshire Post* was right. In the next match at Harrogate, when George Hirst was rested and the inexperienced West Indians bowled Yorkshire out for 50, Sedgwick was so ineffective that at one stage Lebrun Constantine – father of the great Learie – despatched him for five fours in one over. Thus the great Yorkshire side, albeit without Hirst and Haigh, joined newcomers Northamptonshire and an All Scotland eleven as the only teams to lose to the tourists. Sedgwick, nevertheless, was retained in the side for the Roses match at Old Trafford, but he made so little impression in the Lancashire first innings that he did not bowl in the second and never appeared in the Yorkshire side again.

Further south, at Blackheath, the *Times*' suspicions were right, too, as Kent defeated Surrey to leave only 15 percentage points separating the first five in the championship table. There was another month of cricket to be played – and, as the excitement mounted, it would be played in the hottest weather England had known for years.

GEORGE HIRST IN JULY

Date	Opponents	Venue	Batting 1	Batting 2	Bowling Overs	W-R	Overs	W-R
2-4	Gloucs	Headingley	6	10	10	0-23	14	3-27
5-7	Notts	Dewsbury	14	4	12	7-27	24	7-70
12-14	Sussex	Hove	122	15	26.1	3-70	12	1-26
16-18	Derbyshire	Sheffield	89*		9	1-33	10	1-28
19-21	Somerset	Huddersfield	3		13	1-38	28.5	5-86
23-25	Sussex	Bradford	14	42	29	2-115	13	4-21
26-28	Surrey	The Oval	0	87	26	2-53	5	0-10
30-1	Worcs	Hull	37		9.3	5-15	16	3-45

BATTING IN JULY

M	Inns	NO	HS	Runs	Average	100	50
8	13	1	122	443	36.91	1	2

BATTING IN MAY TO JULY

M	Inns	NO	HS	Runs	Average	100	50
24	40	4	169	1556	43.22	4	9

BOWLING IN JULY

Overs	Mdns	Runs	Wkts	Average	10wm	5wi
257.3	48	687	45	15.26	1	4

BOWLING IN MAY TO JULY

Overs	Mdns	Runs	Wkts	Average	10wm	5wi
896.2	208	2277	149	15.28	3	13

CHAMPIONSHIP TABLE – 1 AUGUST

	Played	Won	Drawn	Lost	Points	Percentage
Surrey	20	14	4	2	12	75.00
Yorkshire	21	13	6	2	11	73.33
Kent	15	9	4	2	7	63.63
Lancashire	20	13	4	3	10	62.50
Nottinghamshire	16	8	6	2	6	60.00
Warwickshire	15	6	6	3	3	33.33
Essex	16	5	6	5	0	0.00
Middlesex	10	3	2	5	-2	-25.00
Sussex	15	4	4	7	-3	-27.27
Hampshire	15	4	3	8	-4	-33.33
Worcestershire	13	2	6	5	-3	-42.85
Somerset	14	3	3	8	-5	-45.45
Northamptonshire	14	3	2	9	-6	-50.00
Leicestershire	18	3	3	12	-9	-60.00
Derbyshire	14	2	0	12	-10	-71.42
Gloucestershire	12	1	3	8	-7	-77.77

The Month of August

A heatwave on August Bank Holiday Monday brought crowds to county cricket up and down the land: to The Oval, where Surrey and Nottinghamshire played out a high-scoring draw, to Canterbury where – amid the marquees, the brass bands and the amateur theatricals – Kent made light work of Sussex, and to Old Trafford, where 'the sun shone with almost tropical intensity' on the Roses match and the gates closed before the start with 28,500 spectators inside.

For two days the crowd, who a month earlier had let out 'a huge howl of rejoicing' on hearing of Yorkshire's first defeat, watched in fascination as each side played out its first innings, with Yorkshire finally emerging in front by 11 runs. But the White Rose wilted in the evening of the second day when, in 80 minutes, five wickets went down for 77 and only George Hirst of the top-order batsmen survived for the morning. 'The Lancashire attack was very fine,' *The Times* thought, 'and Hirst was the only man who played a confident game.'

The tropical heat generated a thunderstorm in the early hours of the morning and, with Lancashire scheduled to travel all the way down to Canterbury at the end of the day, the match resumed as early as eleven o'clock, when – on what *Wisden* called 'a more or less ruined wicket' – Hirst soon lost two more partners. At 107 for seven, Yorkshire stood on the verge of a third defeat in their championship campaign.

Yet, as so often when the contest was at its keenest, George Hirst was at his best and, in the view of *Wisden*, he played no finer an innings that summer than he did that morning at Old Trafford. 'It is almost a truism,' the *Yorkshire Post* wrote, 'that no batsman is more capable of forcing runs under difficult conditions than this great-hearted Yorkshireman.' 'He played remarkably well,' said *The Times*. 'He gave a chance when he had made 75, but otherwise his batting was a fine blend of discretion and dash.'

He made 85, Ernest Smith – who the previous August at Leyton had batted an hour for a championship-winning nought not out – 'took many risks' in a bright 46, and suddenly Lancashire were up against Hirst, Rhodes and Haigh on a sticky wicket, wanting 205 for victory.

They were all out for 97, and they fared no better in the next three days at Canterbury. It was a gruelling journey, and so late were they in reaching the city the next morning that play in the match did not get under way till 12.30. A new record attendance of over 13,000 filled the ground, and the designated Ladies' Day created 'a picnic party' atmosphere, with 'gay parties in up-to-date conveyances' and 'all as merry as a marriage-ball'. All, that is, except the Lancashire fielders who, despite the shortened day, found themselves on the receiving end of a Kent score of 409 for three.

By Saturday morning they had lost by an innings and 195 runs, and their championship challenge was over.

Kent, by contrast, had won six championship matches in a row, and they added two more the following week when they travelled west to play at Cheltenham and Taunton. Yorkshire, meanwhile, drew a high-scoring match at Leicester, saw their third and final visit to Headingley as ruined by the weather as the first two and won by an innings against Warwickshire at Harrogate. But the best news for them came from The Oval where Lancashire beat Surrey. Once again, with the race moving into its final fortnight, Yorkshire were in first place in the table.

	Played	*Won*	*Drawn*	*Lost*	*Points*	*Percentage*
Yorkshire	25	15	8	2	13	76.47
Kent	19	13	4	2	11	73.33
Surrey	24	16	5	3	13	68.42
Nottinghamshire	18	9	7	2	7	63.63
Lancashire	24	14	5	5	9	47.36

The next round of matches brought Surrey to Sheffield, and *The Times* tried to calculate the consequences of each possible outcome. 'One thing at least seems certain,' it concluded. 'That is that the county championship competition will retain its interest right up to the very last week of the cricket season.'

By this stage of the summer George Hirst had scored 1,765 runs in 45 innings and taken 170 wickets in 1,035 overs. They were figures that led the *Yorkshire Post* to raise for the first time the prospect – 'with seven possible matches before him' – that Hirst might 'perform a feat which the cricket world has not yet seen.' 2,000 runs and 200 wickets in one summer. 'Such a feat could not be achieved by one more worthy of the honour than the stalwart Yorkshire professional.'

Against Surrey at Bramall Lane he found himself facing the fast bowler Neville Knox with the scoreboard reading 22 for three, and 'he played one of his fine gritty innings', his 47 much the highest score in a Yorkshire total of 144. He made a duck second time round, but he bowled 22 overs in each innings, twice dismissed the prolific Hayward cheaply – the second time with a ball fast enough to ricochet off the stumps and 'travel at a great pace to the boundary' – and his eight wickets helped to give Yorkshire a victory that effectively made the championship a two-horse race with Kent. With only Gloucestershire and Somerset left to play, the Yorkshiremen seemed to have jumped their last demanding hurdle.

The Times, celebrating the dominance of the home-grown teams put out by Kent and Yorkshire, expressed concern at the practice of several of the other counties – taking advantage of the short residential period required for qualification – of importing 'colonial cricketers' at the expense of their own young men. Trott, Tarrant, Roche, Vogler, the list was growing, and *The Times* saw only danger in the trend.

> The practice has increased to such an extent that in some counties the younger professionals are already regretting that they were induced by inferred promises to leave the bench or the mine to seek a living in the cricket field.
>
> County cricket is important and valuable because of the importance and value which it derives from the word county. The county stands for something that is particularly old and particularly English, and in everyday life a man derives advantage or importance merely because his connexion with his county dates back a large number of years. County support is extended to cricket on this principle, and it will surely be withdrawn in proportion as latter-day manipulators toy with or disregard that principle in their desire to overreach the county next door. A fine and healthy institution is not to be turned into a practical farce for the sake of giving personal pleasure to, or conferring financial advantage on, a few individuals. The one object of the county championship competition is to see which county can produce the best cricketers, and not which can purchase the best cricketers. Under the present system a millionaire with a hobby for cricket could make Rutland the champion county in about four years' time, and there need not be a Rutland man in the winning eleven.

The night of Wednesday 22 August, when the Yorkshire cricketers travelled down from Sheffield to Bristol, was said to be the hottest of the year – though it would get hotter still the following week. Their long journey began at Sheffield Station at 4.40 and it ended at Bristol Temple Meads at 9.35.

They were long, gruelling days for the cricketers. George Hirst, when he went back to his own house after a match, would walk home with his bag from the railway station at Mirfield, a two-mile uphill journey that climbed more than 400 feet. However, according to his grand-daughter Margaret, in later life he liked to tell the story of one occasion when he did not walk.

"At the end of one match, wherever they'd been, he was so tired that he hired a carriage, and he sat with his feet out of the carriage window. He took his shoes and socks off to get the air to his feet."

Bill Bowes recalled Hirst telling him how in May he would weigh 13 stone 7 pounds and by August he would be down to 12 stone 12. Hirst also told him about that summer of 1906, about the tiredness he felt in his legs as the season wore on.

George said the muscles of his legs felt like iron, and he had to massage them night and morning with oils. He swore by Neats-foot Oil. He used it right through his career from the time he hurt his leg in Australia, and he was using it thirty years later before going round to the Yorkshire nets for a coaching session.

'I've used gallons of this,' he told me. 'I don't know what I'd 'a done without it. I asked the doctor one day why it was I found it so necessary. All he said was, 'Don't you realise, Mr Hirst, you've given your legs more use than five ordinary men in a lifetime. You're lucky if you can keep them in order with a drop of oil.' 'I suppose, looked at that way, I can't grumble,' said George.

1,812 runs, many of them scored under pressure. 1,079 overs, bowling with a knee that he had to bandage up and off a run which reminded one writer of 'a cork tossed about by little waves on the sea', an action that ought to have left him 'tired out after a dozen overs.' Even the nights at home saw his sleep broken by the cries of his newborn daughter. How George Herbert Hirst, sitting with his pipe in the railway carriage, in the heat of that journey to Bristol, must have longed to put his feet out of the window!

August 1906. Yorkshire's trip to the West Country coincided with a motor tour there by General Booth of the Salvation Army. In Chard he grew irritated by a group of 'fashionably dressed ladies near the platform who fanned themselves owing to the oppressive heat.' "I cannot talk if you persist in fanning yourselves. If you think the weather warm, what must it be for the poor old General who has already spoken three times this morning?" When the ladies got up and left, he accused them of coming only to parade their dresses.

Meanwhile, in Worcester, a commission of enquiry was investigating allegations of irregularity at the General Election earlier in the year. 'A Liberal worker named James Hayes declared that, wherever one went on election day, people wanted money. It was the general cry, and voters hung back till five o'clock to see what they could get. This had always been the case at Worcester.'

For their match at Bristol Yorkshire recalled the fast bowler Billy Ringrose, who had not played since early May, and, in partnership with George Hirst, he soon had a strong Gloucestershire side in trouble at 54 for six. The three gifted amateurs Townsend, Sewell and Jessop all fell to him, and only some late-order runs lifted the home team to 164. Then, in the latter part of the day, on what was agreed to be a good wicket, Yorkshire's batsmen – Hirst among them – lost their way against the beguiling flight of the slow left-armer George Dennett, who a fortnight earlier – on the same ground – had taken all ten Essex wickets.

Dennett took five wickets that evening and three more in the morning when batting had been made more difficult by an overnight storm. Yorkshire finished five runs behind on first innings, and at close of play – with Hirst striking five times in 32 overs and Gloucestershire struggling to 218 for eight – the game seemed in the balance.

Then came Saturday and the climax of a match which, *The Times* reckoned, 'did credit to nearly every individual who took part in it.'

Yorkshire wanted 234 for victory. 'Not a great task for a champion side to face under ordinary conditions,' the Gloucestershire captain Gilbert Jessop wrote, 'but this was no ordinary occasion, for a defeat here meant to Yorkshire the loss of the championship. Their cricket suffered for this knowledge, and many a ball before the crisis began was met with a respect which in other circumstances would have been taken by the scruff of the neck.'

They were 87 for three when Hirst replaced Wilfred Rhodes at the wicket. All over England Hirst had made vital runs for his side that summer, so often seeming to know when to defend and when to attack, and today, with the pitch playing well, he opted for attack. His first scoring shot, a four, went through keeper Board's legs and might have been a catch. Then he made 'a great hit to leg' and might have been caught on the boundary edge by Sewell. Then, still not moderating his approach, he jumped out to drive at a ball from Dennett, hit it high in the air and watched as Jessop, impeded for a moment by a team-mate, held the catch to 'a great shout' from the crowd. For once, the *Bristol Times* thought, 'Hirst could not be complimented for the display he gave.'

A fifth wicket fell seven runs later, but gradually the Yorkshiremen steadied the ship. Horace Rudston of Hull and the acting captain Ernest Smith, who had been to school at nearby Clifton, 'showed splendid defence but missed no opportunity of scoring.'

The excitement was building, and news of the state of the match brought thousands more to the ground after lunch. According to *The Observer* newspaper the next morning, the tension of the contest, with its crucial bearing on the destination of the championship, spread far and wide as 'myriads, just as keenly if not as breathlessly, heard, as it were, the ticking of the electrical agencies bringing the news every few moments throughout the country.'

At 185 for five Yorkshire needed only 49 runs for victory. Smith was then bowled and, before half the remaining runs could be scored, disaster struck not once but twice. First Rudston, cutting a ball from Jessop, stepped back too far and dislodged a bail with his bat. Then, with Jessop again the bowler, Schofield Haigh blocked a ball, only to see it roll backwards and, though it seems that he had time to check its path, 'he stood and watched it do its fatal work.' In fact, 'it shook off the leg bail.' According to the *Western Daily*

Press, 'it was in keeping with the whole character of the game that men should get out so remarkably.'

At 207 for eight the tide was turning the way of Gloucestershire, and it took all the concentration of Hubert Myers – 'always a good bat' – and David Hunter – 'a man of inexhaustible resource and pluck' – to ensure that 'Yorkshire faith was unshaken'. With Hunter happy to play the quieter role, and with both of them 'appealed against several times without success', the score rose to 223 for eight. Just eleven runs were wanted.

At this point Hunter changed his tactics and, 'instead of leaving the runs to Myers he embarked upon the enterprise himself.' Alas, with his first aggressive stroke, he 'lifted straight, but rather low, to Townsend', who not only caught the ball but, in the excitement, threw down the bowler's end stumps as if to run out Myers off the same delivery.

Oh, how on tenterhooks had become the Bristol crowd! Yet such, it seems, was 'their sporting instinct' that 'no stroke during the three days received heartier recognition than the one with which Myers reduced the margin from 11 to 7 when the last man was in.'

The last man was Billy Ringrose, with a nought to his name in the first innings, and Myers tried to keep him off strike. They ran a frantic leg-bye to give Myers the bowling and, in the process, 'the newcomer was nearly run out'. Somewhere, amid all the tension, there was a no ball, then another leg-bye, with another near run-out, to keep Myers on strike to face Dennett. He played out the first five balls, then unaccountably off the sixth he ran two runs – though, in one report, 'judging by his expression when the over was called, he had lost count of the balls.'

So it was two runs to win, one run only for Yorkshire to avoid defeat and thus retain their position at the head of the championship table. Ringrose was on strike, and unexpectedly Jessop himself took the ball. Myers, still upset that he had unnecessarily left himself at the wrong end, 'tried to make amends by walking down the wicket and giving his partner some advice. He even went so far as to show him how to play, for he stood at the crease and made an imaginary stroke or two.'

Jessop took the ball and waited. His intention was to bowl a leg-stump yorker to Ringrose, but it came out wrong and flew down the leg side. One reporter reckoned that Ringrose only had to push out bat or pad to send the ball away for the winning runs, but the other reports all emphasised the near certainty that it would speed away for byes. 'Jessop's face was a study till Board, by an almost superhuman effort, literally flung himself across to stop the byes which would have lost Gloucestershire the game. Then Jessop smiled.'

'The second ball hit Ringrose on the leg, and there was a beseeching sort of appeal to West, the umpire, but without avail.'

Bill 'Pop' West was a well-established umpire, a big man who twenty years earlier had been a heavyweight boxing champion, and all eyes were on him again when the very next delivery from Jessop also hit the hapless Ringrose on the leg. This time the batsmen set off for a leg-bye, the one run that would preserve Yorkshire's championship hopes, but, before they had completed it, West's finger was up and the game was over.

Gloucestershire had won by one run.

'The hit on the leg cost Ringrose no doubt a bruise,' wrote the *Western Daily Press*, 'and his side the championship.'

'The crowd swarmed across the ground. Jessop was the man most of them made for and, in spite of his efforts to escape, he was borne shoulder high to the pavilion. His colleagues received many a handshake and, what they appreciated less, many a hearty slap upon the back from hands that were neither clean nor light.'

It was a game played in the best of spirits, and 'the vanquished champions were amongst the first to congratulate their conquerors.'

The celebrations did not stop once the Gloucestershire team had left the field. 'Thousands assembled in front of the directors' room, and the players one by one were cheered with extraordinary enthusiasm as they appeared at the windows and waved their hands.'

Gilbert Jessop made a speech. 'Although they had heard a great deal in the papers about brightening the game, he did not think it needed any brightening when they could have such cricket as he and the Gloucestershire team had just enjoyed.'

Telegrams of congratulation arrived, 'many of which, strange to say, came from Kent.' Then, after the celebrations had died down, Jessop headed off to the Bristol Rovers' sports day. 'The programme was not half over when he arrived, and it was some little while, so great was the excitement, before the interest of the spectators was again awakened in the sports.'

There were matches still to be played, but the *Western Daily Press* proved to be right. Kent, with a team brimful of confidence, had no alarms in completing their season with their ninth, tenth and eleventh victories in succession, and Yorkshire were left to rue the one run that got away at Bristol.

When the Yorkshire players made their way to Lord Hawke's Wighill Park in the autumn, Hawke's eldest sister is said to have turned to Billy Ringrose. "Tell me, who was the wretched man who got out?" And Ringrose, blushing, confessed, "It was me, ma'am."

The next week would be Ringrose's last as a Yorkshire cricketer but, in a strange coincidence, 26 years later he would come close to leaving the county short of one crucial run for a second time. As the Yorkshire scorer at Leyton, when Holmes and Sutcliffe broke by one run the world record with an opening partnership of 555, he would mislay a no-ball in his scorebook and for some minutes insist that the total was only 554.

One run short. It lowered Yorkshire's championship percentage from 77.77 to 68.42. It was not a system that impressed *The Times*. 'Kent, in the opinion of a great many, are the best side of the year; but they are not the best side of the year just because Gloucestershire beat Yorkshire by one run. They are certainly not today ten per cent better than Yorkshire than they were last Saturday morning.'

WG Grace pitched into the controversy more fiercely. He not only objected to a system that penalised defeat more heavily than it rewarded victory, he also thought it absurd that Yorkshire, by playing 28 matches, had lost to Nottinghamshire while Kent, opting to play only 22 times, had avoided playing them. 'The county championship is simply rotten,' he said, 'and should be improved without delay.' He further argued for two divisions, with promotion and relegation, and for a reduction in the number of matches played, allowing the amateur more opportunity to take part fully, hence 'bringing back a class of player who will not regard it in deadly earnest as his life's business.'

Lord Hawke disagreed, thinking that a separation into two divisions would spell financial ruin for the lesser counties while JT Tyldesley, the Lancashire professional, 'doubted if reducing first-class cricket to the level of a league football competition would be for the good of the game.'

The same argument was being had at club level, with the annual meeting of the Bristol and District Cricket Association debating a proposal to form a local league. The Gloucestershire amateur Charles Townsend, a solicitor who had moved to Stockton-on-Tees to be the town's Official Receiver, spoke in favour of the proposal: "I can unhesitatingly say that the league cricket we play in Stockton on Saturday afternoon is the best club cricket I have ever played." But his motion was defeated, and the Bristol and District Cricket League was not established for another 66 years.

Thus, cricket in 1906 wrestled with arguments that would preoccupy it through much of the century, and a summer which *Wisden* called 'one of the most brilliant of recent years' ended in some controversy.

However, there were matches still to be played and, with the heatwave growing daily more intense, Yorkshire moved on to Bath to play their final championship contest against Somerset. 'The cricket ground is undoubtedly one of the prettiest in the country,' the *Huddersfield Examiner* reported, 'but the surrounding hills, which lend enchantment to the view, have a very oppressive effect upon the atmosphere below.'

On the first day George Hirst scored a chanceless century. The next day, in 'heat that was felt more by the Northerners than by the acclimatised men of the South', he bowled 26 overs and took six wickets for 70. The Yorkshire captain was again Ernest Smith and, preferring to save his bowlers from a double dose of work in 'the extreme heat', he chose not to enforce the follow-on. However his main bowler, George Hirst, found himself back at the crease an hour later, promoted to number three to accelerate the scoring. 'Determined that he should have his batting over to be ready for the bowling' on the third day, he engaged in 'hitting of the most invigorating kind', completing his 50 in 35 minutes, then with a two to leg bringing up his 2,000 runs for the season, 'the feat being greeted with considerable cheering.' Hirst, together with Rhodes, raced on at a great pace. After only an hour at the wicket he had reached 93 when he hit the ball in the air to 'the long field' where the New Zealand-born Old Etonian Peter Johnson ran towards it, only to spill the chance and split a finger.

In the great heat Somerset seemed to have given up the contest, for minutes later – with Hirst on 95 – their captain Lionel Palairet brought himself on to bowl under-arm lobs and, with a four and a single, 'Hirst added to his many great achievements that of scoring two separate hundreds in a match.' Soon afterwards, the wicket-keeper Henry Martyn was asked to bowl, handing over his normal duties to Palairet who kept without gloves.

At the end of a long, hot month, at the end of a long, gruelling championship campaign George Hirst had become only the second Yorkshireman – after David Denton at Trent Bridge in June – ever to make two centuries in a match, and between the two innings, played in blistering heat, he had bowled 26 overs and taken six wickets. The next day he sent down another 15 overs – 'bowling at a great pace' – and took another five wickets, thus becoming the only man ever, in the whole history of cricket, to score two hundreds and take five or more wickets in both innings in the same match. 'It was difficult,' one reporter thought, 'which to admire most, his batting or his bowling. In each department, he was undoubtedly the master. He attacked the bowling of his opponents in the same wholehearted style as he went for their batsmen.'

'A weak leg handicapped him last season,' recalled the *Yorkshire Post*, 'and has several times threatened to do the same this year, but he has persevered with a pluck that is characteristic of the man.'

Now he had 195 wickets in the summer, and his next destination was the Scarborough Festival, where he was due to play for Yorkshire against MCC, for the Players against the Gentlemen and for the North against the South.

The early finish allowed the Yorkshire team to depart Bath Spa station at 3.13 pm on a Midland Railway train that arrived at Sheffield at 7.53. From there they travelled on to York, arriving at 10 o'clock, and, changing again, they reached Scarborough at 11.33. It was a journey of eight hours 20 minutes, and it was made in a sultry atmosphere.

In the English Channel, early the next morning, Tom Burgess of Rotherham set off in his attempt to become the first man since Captain Webb in 1875 to swim all the way to France. But fog descended, and 18 hours later, having swum for 42 miles and been beaten back by fierce currents, he abandoned his task four miles short of the French coast.

At Scarborough at the same time, with the temperature heading towards its highest point for thirty years, George Hirst was bowling another 33 overs against 'the strongest team to represent the MCC this season'. With his second ball he knocked out the off-stump of Archie MacLaren. Then in the same over the Worcestershire captain Henry Foster was dropped at slip, only to be held in the same position in Hirst's next over. That was 197 wickets, and number 198 came before lunch when he bowled Captain 'Teddy' Wynyard.

The South African Vogler made it 199, and that is where his tally stood at tea when perhaps he sat with a quiet gin-and-sherry mix, reflecting on his long summer's work.

All the crowd willed him to 200 wickets, and two elderly ladies among them, the mothers of Rhodes and Hirst, were apparently so overcome by the stress that they went for a walk outside the ground, staying out there beyond the end of the tea interval

Lord Hawke, back in the Yorkshire side for the first time for a month, did not take the field after tea, but his replacement – Henry Foster of the MCC side – stood at short leg and, from the very first ball, bowled by Hirst, 'received an easy catch from a skier by the batsman Braund.'

As Braund departed, offering congratulations as he went, 'Mr Leveson-Gower, who was batting at the bowler's wicket, promptly shook hands with Hirst, and other players around joined in the congratulations, while the crowd gave a most cordial round of cheering.' In the street outside, Mrs Rhodes and Mrs Hirst knew what it signified.

Hirst had taken 200 wickets, one of only five occasions when a Yorkshire bowler has achieved this feat purely in Yorkshire matches, the others being Wilfred Rhodes in 1900 and in 1901, George Macaulay in 1925 and Bob Appleyard in 1951. But none of them scored even 1,000 runs in the season.

"I was absolutely jiggered after what I'd done," recalls Bob Appleyard, whose run tally was just 104. "How he had the energy to bat as well, I can't imagine."

From Allerton Hall, Leeds came a letter to Hirst from the Honourable FS Jackson. 'As long as the likes of you are forthcoming,' he wrote, 'and they play in the same spirit as they have always done, cricket is bound to flourish in Yorkshire.'

On Saturday, while Kent were sealing their championship with an innings victory at Bournemouth, George Hirst batted for Yorkshire for the last time that summer. With his team chasing 287, he hit a six and eleven fours in an unbeaten, 50-minute innings of 76 that carried off 'the comparatively rare' achievement of winning a victory against a declaration.

Cricket Match, YORKSHIRE versus M. C. C. & Ground

FIRST INNINGS OF M. C. C. & Ground — Umpires { V. A. Titchmarsh / W. Oakley

Order of going in	BATSMAN	RUNS AS SCORED	HOW OUT	BOWLER	Total Runs
1	R.H. Spooner	41111444414424411441111414114444	Bld	Rhodes	47
2	A.C. MacLaren		Bld	Hirst	0
3	H.K. Foster		C. Smith	Hirst	0
4	F.L. Fane	11114134111143144444421111211131111	C. Tunnicliffe	Rhodes	67
5	M.W. Payne		Bld	Rhodes	0
6	Capt. Wynyard	1411131	Bld	Hirst	13
7	Braund	1111211111114414111142211311111211244414241 1	C. Sub	Hirst	73
8	Thompson	3122142111111	C. Hunter	Myers	20
9	Vogler	11441114411111	Bld	Hirst	25
10	H.D.G. Leveson Gower	1311421442142314444 1	Not	out	50
11	G.G. Napier	111141112	C. Myers	Rhodes	18

BYES [ ] LEG BYES / [1] NO BALLS // [2] WIDES [ ] 3

Runs at the fall of each wicket	1 for	2 for	3 for	4 for	5 for	6 for	7 for	8 for	9 for	10 for	TOTAL
	0	6	138	138	151	161	219	266	295	346	346
Batsman No	2	3	1	5	4	6	8	9	7	11	

BOWLING ANALYSIS—FIRST INNINGS.

NUMBER OF "OVERS" AND "RUNS" MADE FROM EACH BOWLER.

BOWLERS	No. Balls	Wides	1	2	3	4	5	6	7	8	9	10	11	12	13	14
Hirst	1		W....	1W..1.	1	..3...	1	......	4.4...	..41.3	411...	.4.44	1.111.	W....	......	1....
			.22...	...11.	1.....	...12.	...41.	1.1...	....4.	.1112.	.1...0.	1..1W	14....	......	4.21..	W.....
			42.1..	1.2...3	.14...	4.1..4	41....									
Ringrose			.4.1..	.1.11.	.4...1	41....	..1...	..11.1	....4.	..14...	...1.					
Rhodes			4..24.	4.1...	.121...	..1.11	114...	11...4	444WW.	..41.1	.W...1	31..1	......	.3..21	.1..1	.1....
			......	.1...4	..4.1.	.111..	....4.	......	.4...	4.4..	..1...	.11.1.	.2W			
Haigh			444...	...1..	......	....2.	..1111	3...1	11.1..	......	1...1.	......	31....	....1..	111.44	
Myers	1		......	.1....	22....	......	1....	.....W	11.1..	21..1	44.104	..14.	4...2	.3111.	1.....	

	BOWLERS	Overs	Maidens	Runs	Wickets	No Balls	Wides
1	Hirst	33	5	124	5	1	
2	Ringrose	9	0	32	0		
3	Rhodes	24.3	3	102	4		
4	Haigh	13	3	41	0		
5	Myers	13	3	44	1	1	
6							
7							
8							
9							
10							

It was a golden end to a golden summer, and it took place in weather so hot that, away in Manchester on that Saturday, on the first day of the football season, two of the Manchester City players – 'having retired before the interval on account of the great heat' – did not reappear for the second half of their First Division match against Woolwich Arsenal. The visitors won 4-1 and, according to the *Yorkshire Post*, three more City players also retired in the second half, leaving their side with just six men on the field.

Hirst played the following week at Scarborough and, after that, the four-day match at The Oval when the Rest of England beat the Champion County Kent. His final tally for the summer was 2,385 runs and 208 wickets, and *Wisden* paid tribute:

> Only a very strong man in perfect health would have been equal to the mere physical labour involved, but Hirst thrives on hard work, and at the end of the season he was so fresh and well that nobody seeing him bat or bowl could have guessed that any extra demands had been made upon him. Indeed, he bowled in quite his finest form when the Rest of England beat Kent at The Oval in September, the last fixture of the year.

He was asked if anybody would ever match his achievement. "If they do," he said with a smile, "they'll be very tired."

It was a line that Fred Trueman borrowed, adding an adjective or two, when he took his 300th Test wicket. Time has proved Trueman wrong, as the merry-go-round of modern Test cricket has seen bowlers go past 500 and 600 Test wickets.

But time has left George Herbert Hirst and his summer of 1906 on its own. A summer without equal.

GEORGE HIRST IN AUGUST

Date	*Opponents*	*Venue*	*Batting*		*Bowling*			
			1	*2*	*Overs*	*W-R*	*Overs*	*W-R*
6-8	Lancashire	Old Trafford	4	85	26.3	5-67	12	2-29
9-11	Leics	Leicester	23		36	2-76	6	0-19
13-15	Middlesex	Headingley	29		27	3-64	5	3- 8
16-18	Warwicks	Harrogate	68		18.4	6-30	8	0-18
20-22	Surrey	Sheffield	47	0	21.5	3-69	22	4-50
23-25	Gloucs	Bristol	13	12	17	2-36	32	5-74
27-29	Somerset	Bath	111	117*	26	6-70	15	5-45
30-1	MCC	Scarborough	23	76*	33	5-124	9	1-33

BATTING IN AUGUST

M	*Inns*	*NO*	*HS*	*Runs*	*Average*	*100*	*50*
8	13	2	117*	608	55.27	2	3

BATTING IN MAY TO AUGUST – HIS YORKSHIRE SEASON

M	*Inns*	*NO*	*HS*	*Runs*	*Average*	*100*	*50*
32	53	6	169	2164	46.04	6	12

BOWLING IN AUGUST

Overs	*Mdns*	*Runs*	*Wkts*	*Average*	*10wm*	*5wi*
315	55	812	52	15.61	1	6

BOWLING IN MAY TO AUGUST – HIS YORKSHIRE SEASON

Overs	*Mdns*	*Runs*	*Wkts*	*Average*	*10wm*	*5wi*
1211.2	263	3089	201	15.36	4	19

GEORGE HIRST IN SEPTEMBER

Date	*Fixture*	*Venue*	*Batting*		*Bowling*			
			1	*2*	*Overs*	*W-R*	*Overs*	*W-R*
3-5	North v South	Scarborough	84		13	0-59	13	0-37
6-8	Players v Gents	Scarborough	6	53	14	1-48	7	0-49
10-13	Rest v Kent	The Oval	61	17	29	2-79	19	4-73

FINAL FIGURES FOR SUMMER

BATTING

M	*Inns*	*NO*	*HS*	*Runs*	*Average*	*100*	*50*
35	58	6	169	2385	45.86	6	15

BOWLING

Overs	*Mdns*	*Runs*	*Wkts*	*Average*	*10wm*	*5wi*
1306.2	272	3434	208	16.50	4	19

FINAL CHAMPIONSHIP TABLE

	Played	*Won*	*Drawn*	*Lost*	*Points*	*Percentage*
Kent	22	16	4	2	14	77.77
Yorkshire	28	17	8	3	14	70.00
Surrey	28	18	6	4	14	63.63
Lancashire	26	15	5	6	9	42.85
Nottinghamshire	20	9	7	4	5	38.46
Warwickshire	20	7	9	4	3	27.27
Essex	22	9	7	6	3	20.00
Hampshire	20	7	4	9	-2	-12.50
Gloucestershire	20	6	4	10	-4	-25.00
Sussex	24	6	6	12	-6	-33.33
Middlesex	18	4	4	10	-6	-42.85
Northamptonshire	18	4	4	10	-6	-42.85
Somerset	16	4	2	10	-6	-42.85
Worcestershire	20	2	10	8	-6	-60.00
Leicestershire	22	3	5	14	-11	-64.70
Derbyshire	20	2	1	17	-15	-78.94

The later years

Though George Hirst had turned 35 when the summer of 1906 ended, he played through each of the next eight years, up to the outbreak of the Great War. He completed the double of 1,000 runs and 100 wickets comfortably in all of them bar the last, and in 1908 and 1912 he played again in championship-winning Yorkshire sides. He declined to tour with England again, but in 1909 in the Edgbaston Test he and Kent's slow left-armer Colin Blythe took all twenty wickets between them as they bowled out Australia for 74 and 151.

After the War he played three more summers of first-class cricket, his last day being at Scarborough in September 1921, on his fiftieth birthday. He was captain of the Players against the Gentlemen and, though he bowled only three overs in the match, he took the final two wickets that brought victory to his side. Apart from a comeback match of no great distinction eight years later on the same ground, that was the end.

"We want George Hirst," the crowd chanted, and he appeared on the pavilion balcony. In the words of AA Thomson, 'Never was his natural dignity, his absolute freedom from self-consciousness, plainer to see. His voice, when he spoke, was clear and firm.'

> Ladies and gentlemen, I'd like to call you the cricketing public. I thank you for your kindness to me. A person always knows his limitations, and I'm not such a good man as you make me out to be.
>
> If I've had any broad views on what they call the game of life, I've learnt them on the cricket field. I've loved many games, but I've been a bit more efficient at cricket. From an unselfish point of view, it's the best game.
>
> What can you have better than a nice green field, with the wickets set up, and to go out and do the best for your side? I leave first-class cricket to those who have got to come. I hope they'll have the pleasure in it that I have had.

He lived for another 33 years. For many summers he was the cricket professional at Eton College – where, in the words of one Old Etonian, contrasting him with the less successful Wilfred Rhodes at Harrow, 'he never put a little toe-nail wrong.'

Among those who played in his cricket elevens at Eton were the Honourable R.F. Wood, son of Lord Halifax, and the Sheepshanks brothers, one of whom played once for Yorkshire before being killed in the Spanish Civil War. But the young Etonian who in later life would make the most lasting impact on the English game was Brian Johnston, the broadcaster whose cheerful voice on *Test Match Special* would become such a characteristic part of the English summer.

Johnston, a schoolboy wicket-keeper, wrote of Hirst:

> He had a sweet disposition and was loved by all the boys. I used to keep wicket to his bowling and even got a stumping on the leg side off him, much to our mutual satisfaction. Even in those days, aged 60, he bowled a lively medium-pace and swung the bowl prodigiously.

Johnston was never in fact a member of the Eton eleven. He would have played in 1931, except that the previous summer's keeper – despite being well past his 19th birthday – had stayed on an extra year. George Hirst, recognising the enthusiasm of the young man, did his best to lessen the disappointment.

> He took me under his wing, and at the Eton and Harrow match at Lord's he took me around with him, to the dressing rooms and even up to the scorer's box at the top of the grandstand.

"George Hirst had a very big influence on my father," Brian's son Barry recalls. "He introduced him to Lord's, and from that day on my father loved the place. It was his greatest regret that he never played there, but he always spoke with affection about George Hirst."

Hirst also coached pre-season at Headingley, both the senior players and the promising youngsters who were picked out to attend in their Easter holidays. Among the boys in 1939 were two future stalwarts of the county, Johnny Wardle and Ted Lester, and, though 67 years have passed, Ted – then a 16-year-old schoolboy from Scarborough – still remembers the kindly welcome he received.

> It was a long way from Scarborough, and I went into the dressing room, not knowing a soul. The first thing he said was, 'Come over here and sit with the other boys.' There were about four of them, sitting in front of the fire, and he made me feel welcome. A lot of coaches would just have ignored me. 'It's not my job to make him feel at home.'
>
> If he asked a young player how they had done in a match, he would never say 'How many did you get?' but 'Did you get any?' It made it far easier to answer if you'd made a low score.
>
> He was the best coach I ever met, mainly because he coached common sense. He didn't try to alter your style; he coached what was there. He once said to me, 'Have you been getting out lbw?' I said, 'No.' So he said, 'All right, then. Just carry on.' Years after, when I went to Lilleshall on a coaching course, I realised what he'd meant. I hit the ball a little bit across the line, through wide mid-on, when I should really have played it straight. He said, 'Carry on,' and it got me hundreds of runs over the

George Hirst at Headingley.
Second from left is Johnny Wardle, second from right is Ted Lester.

years. The present-day coaches would have told me to play straight down the wicket.

He asked me one time how I'd been getting out. I told him I'd been run out in three of my last five innings. 'Send 'em back,' was his advice. Brief and to the point.

He was a wonderful fellow. I think one of the reasons Yorkshire were so good before the war was because of George Hirst's coaching. I've never met anybody who's said a wrong word about him.

'I shall always think of him as the ideal coach,' Len Hutton wrote. 'He was a "natural" one, the guide, philosopher and friend of every young fellow who had a trial under him. I trembled with emotion when I first came face to face with him. Not that he scared me in any way. He was too genial, too happy for that, as though the sun itself had burned into his spirit as well as his limbs. He made me feel that I was better than I was."

"He was an encourager," Margaret his grand-daughter says. "But he would say straight. He would say if he thought you were doing something foolish. I ask my children what they remember of him, and they say, 'His eyes twinkled, and he had highly polished boots.'"

"If a young man came and asked him if he could make a living at cricket," her husband Ronnie recalls, "he would say, 'Have you got a proper job? So, if the lad said, 'I'd like to train as an accountant,' he'd say, 'Unless you're absolutely the tops, be an accountant and enjoy club cricket at the weekend. To make anything of cricket as a living, you've got to be really great.' And he would infer, 'Like I was', though he would never say it."

"We were taught," Margaret says, "if somebody said, 'You played well,' to push it aside. 'Oh, it was nothing.' My grandfather was a nice man, a quiet man. He wasn't a showman. I do remember somebody coming up to him and saying how pleased he was to meet him. And my grandfather said to us afterwards, 'Well, I was the best, you see.' It was just said, as if he were saying, 'Those are daffodils.' There was no boasting."

Each year George Herbert Hirst returned to Scarborough for the Festival, staying in Trafalgar Square overlooking the ground, and each year, as he walked to his seat, the crowd stood up and clapped him.

He died in May 1954, at the age of 82, and Yorkshire that day were at Bristol, where the flag flew at half mast and the two teams stood for a minute in silence. 'Always he played cricket true to himself,' Jim Kilburn wrote in the *Yorkshire Post*, 'happy, earnest and unselfconscious. In the noontime he was ready to bat, bowl or field; in the evening he enjoyed a pipe and a pint and talk of cricket.'

"According to my mother," Margaret says, "one of the last things he said was 'pipe'."

Did he die of any particular illness?

Ronnie offers an answer. "He said to me that he was tired."

Perhaps the last words he would have liked to say were the words he found on the balcony that day at Scarborough:

> What can you have better than a nice green field, with the wickets set up, and to go out and do the best for your side? I leave first-class cricket to those who have got to come. I hope they'll have the pleasure in it that I have had.